# The Last Prom

## *Sydney Gardens*
## *Bath*

## Brenda Snaddon

Millstream Books

A Tea Garden, an engraving by George Morland of a scene in the Barley Mow Tea Gardens, Islington, about 1786. The family group sits in the shade of a tree, while the waiter pours boiling water into a tea-pot. As they bustled about the gardens carrying their kettles, the waiters would cry, *"Ware kettle! Ware scaldings!"*.

First published in June 2000 by Millstream Books, 18 The Tyning, Widcombe, Bath BA2 6AL

Set in Times New Roman and printed in Great Britain by The Jensen Press, Yeovil, Somerset

© Brenda Snaddon 2000

ISBN 0948975598

A catalogue record for this book is available from the British Library

# Contents

# Introduction

Sydney Gardens is a miraculous survivor. It is now over 200 years ago that Thomas Baldwin laid out the boat-shaped Pleasure Garden on the sloping hillside at the end of Great Pulteney Street. Succeeding generations have made many alterations to suit changing circumstances, most of them regrettable and some of them now irreversible.

The canal still "*contributes to the variety and beauty of this enchanting spot*", and is much drawn and photographed. Main-line trains, rushing through the cutting, at least provide something startlingly different from the ordinary run of city parks. The two buildings at either end of the main Walk are drastically altered and blocked off from each other in uncaring denial of the principal view-line. Large houses have been built on the margins, their gardens encroaching on the park. Modern sports facilities introduce their sharp, hard rectangles into what were once soft-edged and irregular lawns and shrubberies. Already by Victorian times one writer's opinion was that the Gardens were "*a poor shadow of themselves,*" due to "*the sad havoc of modern improvements*".

This short history describes how such compromises have come about, and gives due emphasis to what the Gardens looked like when they were new. Sydney Gardens was the work of four superb designers: Thomas Baldwin, Charles Harcourt Masters, John Rennie and Isambard Kingdom Brunel, three of whom can be placed among the country's finest. It was a good idea, beautifully carried out, and it has survived into our crowded times. Not only that, but there may now be a more cheerful future in store, given the new climate of respect for historic garden styles.

**The Promenade at Sydney Gardens**, by John Nixon, 1801, looking towards Sham Castle on top of the hill. Note the row of dining cubicles and the swing-boats for two people, centre left.

4

# The Background

18th-century pleasure gardens developed naturally from the custom of social walking, or promenading as it was called. Many English towns had walks or avenues of evenly spaced trees, usually on the outskirts in order to benefit from fresh air and country views, and specially planted to create a dignified framework for this formal socialising. Refreshments were sold and sometimes there was background music. In Bath the company gathered in the Grove (now Orange Grove), which was planted with rows of trees, before the triangle of land at river level which is now Parade Gardens was made into formal walks of lime trees in 1708. Gradually the public wanted the comfort of full sit-down meals and soon they got concerts and firework displays as well, following the example of the large London pleasure gardens at Vauxhall and Ranelagh. Bath had the well-loved Spring Gardens, next to Pulteney Weir, opened before 1740 and lasting for 60 years.

Sydney Gardens was a new concept. It embodied the same tradition of an exclusive promenade with entertainments, but also played the part of a green open space in the centre of an elegant scheme of terraced houses. The intention was that from the upper windows, the owners could survey the park-like scenery as if it were their own private grounds. This plan, drawn up by Thomas Baldwin, architect to the Pulteney family who owned the estate, was part of the development of the manor of Bathwick, the hitherto empty land on the east bank of the Avon. Only one of Baldwin's terraces was completed before financial problems overtook the scheme in 1793. A second, by John Pinch the elder, was built by 1808, but by then fashion had begun to turn away from terraces in favour of small villas, and the remainder of the scheme was not implemented.

But Great Pulteney Street, broad and straight, the backbone of the design, and the Gardens to which it makes such an imposing approach, were both completed, and can still be enjoyed today.

**A Sydney Gardens silver token.** These were issued to each shareholder, to be used as free passes into the Pleasure Garden. The Friends of the Holburne Museum now own the original dies used in the casting of these tokens.

# The Original Layout

The Gardens opened in May 1795, heralded by the publication of Charles Harcourt Masters' plan of Bath in January the same year. In spite of its small scale the extract below shows enough detail of the original garden to give a good idea of what it was intended to look like. At the lower end nearest to the city (to the left on the plan) is the Tavern building, known as Sydney House, containing dining rooms and meeting rooms. Next, a wide circular area half enclosed by the two arms of dining cubicles, where the main activities of meeting friends, promenading in fine clothes and taking convivial meals where one could see and be seen, were skilfully catered for. There is also a movable orchestra, a platform in sections, which could be wheeled aside if necessary, and a "*space for fireworks*". From here the main Walk rises eastwards up the slope, ending with a small curved building at the far end, the Loggia.

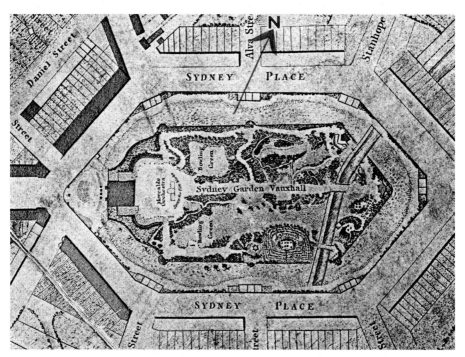

**Sydney Gardens**; an extract from Charles Harcourt Masters' Plan of Bath, issued on 1st January 1795. This shows the canal, added to the later edition of 1810, and also the terrace of New Sydney Place by Pinch the elder. The rest of the terraces and the proposed radiating streets were not built. The Labyrinth can be seen, the swings and the "*Space for Fireworks*". The castle is at the top right corner. The Ride, on the extreme outside edge, encircles the border of rough pasture. The Tavern here is Baldwin's design, which was turned down in favour of Harcourt Masters' more modest building.

In contrast to this wide Walk with its clear vista up to the Loggia, there were also narrower pathways winding away on both sides, often passing through shrubbery so that their destination is concealed. The *New Bath Guide* (1801) describes them as, "*serpentine walks, which at every turn meet with sweet shady bowers furnished with handsome seats, some canopied by Nature, others by Art*": that is, some seats are placed beneath arbours of climbing plants, while others have a man-made roof of wood or tiles. There were areas of lawn, some enclosed by shrubbery like the north Bowling Green, and others left open to permit distant views. There were "*small, delightful groves*", and "*pleasant vistoes*". There were waterfalls and pavilions, also alcoves where parties could sit to take tea, enjoying meanwhile, the "*elegant scenes*" in "*this Elysian field*".

J.C. West, Jun.ʳ Lithog. *The Labyrinth, in Sydney Gardens, Bath.*
*The dotted line denotes the path to be pursued.*

The Frontispiece to John Kerr's *Syllabus or Descriptive Representation*, etc., a guidebook to Sydney Gardens, published in 1825. On the left, the Miller's Wheel and Entrance to Grotto; on the right, the Castle Ruin and Hermit's Cot.

There would also have been urns and statues, which cannot be seen on the plan. But the swings are visible, indicated by groups of four posts in a square, and the Labyrinth is obvious, "*twice as large as Hampton Court's*". Somewhere close by was a moss-covered Grotto from which an underground passage led to the centre of the Labyrinth, where a revolving wheel swing offered an exciting ride high above the hapless wanderers, lost in the maze below. At the top north-east corner is the Castle Ruin with its moat, and a long funnel of lawn in front, allowing it to be seen from the main Walk. This view-line or "*visto*", continues across the south Bowling Green to the far opposite corner of the Gardens, producing a dramatic view of the ivy-covered folly on its promontory, backed by tall trees full of sinister cawing rooks. Such contrived view-lines were greatly admired at the time. So also, was the softer overall style of this garden, which replaced the mid-18th-century lay-outs of London's Vauxhall and Bath's Spring Gardens, now out of date with their grid-like systems based on rigid straight lines. In Sydney Gardens, as the *Bath Guide* told its readers, "*the style is quite new and exhibits the most pleasing variety*".

The artificialities of the gardens are set off by a wide border of rough meadow, a deliberate juxtaposition of 'Art' and 'Nature'; and outside this a Ride, forming "*a healthy and fashionable airing for Gentlemen and Ladies on horseback free from the inconvenience of dirt in winter and dust in summer and not incommoded by carriages of any kind*". The weather-proof surface was achieved by compacting layers of small stones into a hard mass, the same system later used by John McAdam, but known locally some years earlier[1].

The Ride weaves its way past seven small buildings on the perimeter: these were pairs of small houses with a gateway or exit between, called "*Outletts*" by Baldwin, and designed so that large crowds could leave easily after a Gala evening, as well as forming pleasing terminations to the perspective views along the proposed streets leading off Sydney Gardens. Neither "*Outletts*" nor streets were constructed. A border of shrubbery can be

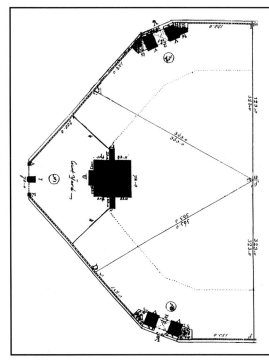

### Baldwin's Plan

Sydney Gardens, the western section of Baldwin's outline plan on the indenture dated 30th September 1794. None of the buildings shown was constructed. His Tavern is 74 feet wide and 79 deep. At the entrance 'J' was a lodge about 10 feet wide with a decorated obelisk rising from it, while 'A' and 'E' were plinths supporting elegant vases. Two of the 'Outletts' are seen, each square house with a tiny area of garden to the side, and a ground-floor passage to allow the exit of crowds after Gala evenings. The dotted line indicates the screen of trees and bushes between the gardens and the rough pasture. *(Bath Records Office)*

made out just inside the boundary wall – some extant trees in this position probably belong to the original planting, notably the large beeches, horse chestnuts and Norway maples.

There were, of course, no herbaceous borders *à la* Gertrude Jekyll, and no beds of Hybrid Tea Roses in this garden. Flowering plants in 1795 were placed in ones and twos on the wavy edges of shrubberies, or in summer, in pots close to buildings. Roses would be mingled with other perennials like cistus, peony or hollyhocks, backed with high shrubs like philadelphus, with accents provided by the thin spires of Italian Cypress. The shrubberies, mostly of evergreens like arbutus (strawberry tree), phillyrea, or holly, would be mixed with blossom trees like bird cherry, cornelian cherry or almond. Climbing roses would be used with other climbers like honeysuckle, everlasting pea, and virgin's bower (clematis).

The whole Garden was walled, as it is today, but with iron railings at the lower end facing Great Pulteney Street. The only entrance was at this end. Visitors walked through the Sydney House building, which stands on the axis of the symmetrical layout. Those on horseback entered the Ride through gates at equidistant points either side of the building. Thus the people became part of the design: ushered in through the Tavern, welcomed by the generous promenade between the dining boxes, and drawn up the slope of the main Walk by the compelling arrangement of the vista, where the charming Loggia is glimpsed, but not seen in its entirety, until one has almost reached it.

Baldwin's design is transitional. Aided by the sloping site and the hilly surroundings, he made a picturesque garden, after the fashionable wavy, relaxed and apparently natural manner that was being applied to large estates in the 1790s by the great Humphry Repton, who was active at Blaise near Bristol in the very year that Sydney Gardens opened. Yet this wayward plan exists within a totally geometric framework, looking back to the formal ideas of a century before. The same juxtaposition is seen in John Eveleigh's Grosvenor Gardens in Bath, set up two years before Sydney Gardens[2]. There is evidence that formality was considered appropriate for town gardens long after it faded from popularity in country estates. (See the restored Georgian garden behind No.4 The Circus, Bath.)

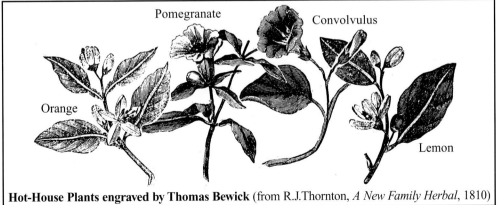

Pomegranate
Convolvulus
Orange
Lemon

**Hot-House Plants engraved by Thomas Bewick** (from R.J.Thornton, *A New Family Herbal*, 1810)

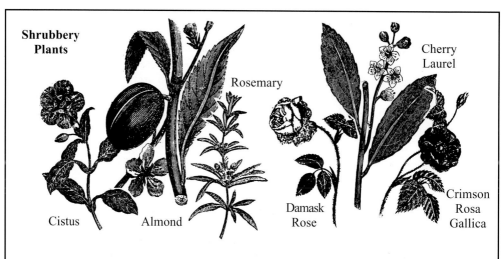

**Shrubbery Plants**

Rosemary

Cherry Laurel

Cistus

Almond

Damask Rose

Crimson Rosa Gallica

**Garden Plants engraved by Thomas Bewick**
(from R.J.Thornton, *A New Family Herbal*, 1810)

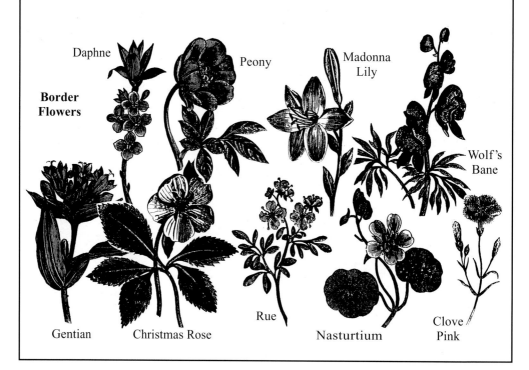

Daphne

Peony

Madonna Lily

**Border Flowers**

Wolf's Bane

Gentian

Christmas Rose

Rue

Nasturtium

Clove Pink

# The Setting Up and Authorship of the Gardens

Work began in December 1792, when Baldwin advertised for masons to construct the boundary wall. In September of the next year the first tree was planted, by way of a publicity event. Unfortunately the financial crisis of that year claimed Baldwin as one of many bankrupts, so that he could no longer be employed as the Estate's architect. Charles Harcourt Masters was the replacement, officially taken on in October 1794, when his new design for a Tavern building was accepted. It is a more compact building than Baldwin's, being of similar width but only half as deep[3].

By this time nearly two years' work had been done on the garden. Starting from scratch on the bare hillside, drains would have been laid, streambeds and underground conduits constructed to manage water from several springs in the upper part of the site. Then there was the laying out of the basic framework of paths and sowing of grass areas, as well as the planting of trees and shrubs. It was, in fact, almost complete by October 1794, and opened to the public six months later, in May 1795.

It opened without its principal building, as Harcourt Masters' Tavern was not begun until November 1796, after two summer seasons had elapsed. Masters is often credited with the design of the garden also, but as he was not appointed until it was almost finished, this claim cannot be upheld. Further, his own map of Bath, on page 6, shows Baldwin's Tavern, not his own. As this map was issued on New Year's Day 1795, it must have been sent to the London engravers soon after the middle of 1794, some months before any decision was made regarding a replacement for the bankrupt Baldwin.

The substitution of Masters' name for Baldwin's was in place from the start, and has remained so, apparently unquestioned, ever since. For example:

> "*This pleasure garden was designed by Mr. Harcourt Masters, architect, in which he has displayed much taste and judgement.*"[4]

> "*...an elegant specimen of the taste of Mr. Masters, who laid out the grounds.*"[5]

Why was this done? Because Sydney Gardens, as a new venture dependent on the custom of respectable citizens, could not afford to be associated with a bankrupt, especially one who had also suffered dismissal from his posts with the Bath Corporation and the Bath Improvement Commission, due to his dishonest conduct of their finances.[6] Yet Baldwin's design for the Tavern had been endorsed by the Committee as late as February 1794, five months into his bankruptcy, and there seems to have been an intention to construct it, until a sudden decision in April brought a halt to the process.[7] The reasons were probably financial, following the collapse of the banks in 1793, but it gave the Committee a chance to revise the design, and include a colonnade and raised orchestra platform on the garden front. They also took the opportunity to engage a new, blameless architect, and thereby expunge Baldwin's name altogether from Sydney Gardens.

Although Masters' building takes up half the ground area of Baldwin's, its front elevation is visually more massive, and changes the nature of the Pulteney Street vista

## The Two Designs for the Hotel or Tavern

*Elevation for the west Front of Vaux Hall and Ranelagh House*

Baldwin's drawing of the elevation of his Hotel, shown in the plans on pages 6 and 8. The building is seven bays wide and seven deep. What appear to be side wings are in fact corridors, set half way down each side. There is an attic storey in the roof space. Visually, this would have been a gentler culmination to the Pulteney Street vista.

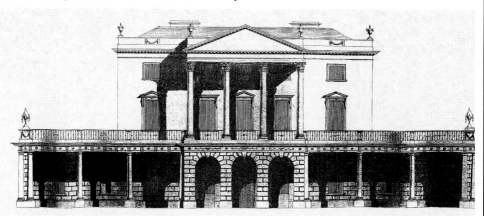

Charles Harcourt Masters' drawing of the elevation of his Hotel building from the Indenture dated 2nd October 1794. This design was constructed, without the loggia, the foundation stone being laid on 16th November 1796. It is the first building known to have been designed by Masters. Before this he had been a surveyor, although the seven years he spent making a 30 feet:1 inch scale model of Bath must have provided an excellent training in architecture. *(Bath Records Office)*

from what Baldwin originally conceived. Masters' grand order portico stands on three rusticated arches, the building rests on an important ground-floor loggia, and there are three floors, plus an attic behind a solid balustrade. It is bold, equal in height to the terraces of Great Pulteney Street, and as imposing as the Guildhall, which it closely resembles. Baldwin's, on the other hand, would have created a gentler termination to the vista, hinting at the pastoral pleasures that lay beyond. His portico, resting at ground level, appears to compress the two storeys, while a third floor is concealed in the roof. The two wings, actually corridors, are set four bays back, and would have been almost invisible as part of the façade.

It would have been, in fact, another of Baldwin's explorations of the mysterious effects of placing a low building at the end of a tall-sided vista, already done in 1787 with the Cross Bath and Bath Street. Here, the Cross Bath appears more distant than it really is because its height does not match the roof-line of the colonnades, although the effect is rather spoilt by the cliff-like façade behind. A similar illusion at the end of Great Pulteney Street would have been especially suitable for a pleasure garden; but the subtlety of the effect would doubtless have been spoilt by the addition, sooner or later, of an extra storey as indeed happened with Masters' Tavern in 1836.

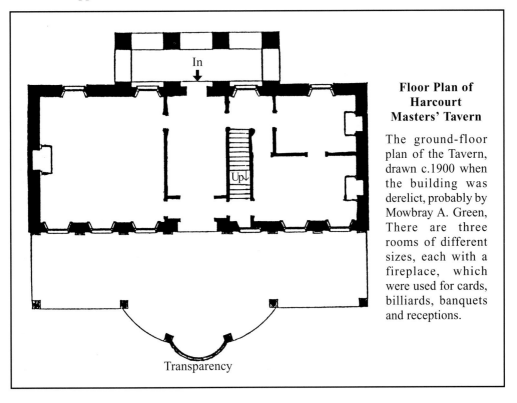

**Floor Plan of Harcourt Masters' Tavern**

The ground-floor plan of the Tavern, drawn c.1900 when the building was derelict, probably by Mowbray A. Green, There are three rooms of different sizes, each with a fireplace, which were used for cards, billiards, banquets and receptions.

# How the Tavern and Gardens Were Managed

The enterprise was funded by the sale of shares, and built on land leased from the Pulteneys. On 29th September 1792 the original agreement was signed, stating that the lease was for 99 years at an annual rent of £142.5s., payable quarterly to Henrietta Laura Pulteney, Baroness Bath, who had inherited her mother's lands and fortune, and administered them with the aid of her father William Johnstone Pulteney. There were 40 shareholders at the outset, plus two treasurers and five trustees. Each share cost £100, to be paid in ten instalments. Shareholders received a silver token to be used as a free pass into the Gardens. Any profits, once all construction work was complete, were to be divided between the shareholders, and paid half-yearly. A committee of seven was to be elected, and changed annually.[8]

A tenant was appointed to take charge of running the Tavern and Pleasure Gardens. His responsibilities included all the catering; the arranging and advertising of all the functions, including detailed announcements of the evening Galas, which were held four or more times each summer; keeping the grounds in good order, which meant from time to time radical refurbishment such as the re-gravelling of all the paths; and also the setting up of completely new attractions like the Cascade in 1810 and the Aviary in 1824. The precise financial arrangements for tenants are not known; whether they kept all the season's takings, whether the committee helped to pay for occasional large items, and so on. It seems that the tenant's own furnishings and catering equipment were used, as there are several occasions when a tenant suddenly leaves, and there is an auction sale of his entire domestic effects, from his tea equipage and venison dish, down to his candle-sticks and gravy spoons, to quote one example, and, in the cellar, "*500 dozen of various foreign wines*".[9]

The tenant set the admission charges. For the first season, 1795, these were: 6d. per person, and 6d. for tea. Subscribers, 2s.6d. per month, 5s. for three months, and 7s.6d. for the whole season. For walking, plus use of the Bowling Greens, l0s. Subscriptions for the Ride were the same. By 1810 there were small increases, and subscriptions for reading the Bath and London papers in the coffee room were 5s.

The charge of 6d. for tea included the services of a waiter who, in fine weather, would bring the tea to any corner of the Gardens. Carrying in one hand a tray of cups and saucers and a tea-pot containing a measure of dry tea, he would have a kettle of boiling water in the other hand, thus producing a fresh brew, however far from the kitchens the party were sitting. This scene is shown in George Morland's engraving of the Barley Mow Tea Gardens, Islington, on page 2.[10]

As well as ordinary Promenades to the music of "*Horns and Clarionets*", Sydney Gardens held Public Breakfasts, usually costing 2s. per person, at which tea, coffee, rolls and Sally Lunns were served at about midday, followed by dancing. At one Public Breakfast in 1799, the Chronicle reports that,

*"The company entered into the spirit of the morning's rural recreation; country dances commenced, and continued till nearly 4 in the afternoon, when the approach of the dinner hour dispersed as elegant and happy a party as ever assembled."* Large private parties were requested to arrange breakfasts in advance, so that the tenant *"may know how to provide"*.

Breakfasts, coffee-drinking, newspaper-reading and card-playing all took place in the ground-floor rooms of the Tavern, which were ready for use in the summer of 1799. The Ballroom is not mentioned until 1801, being described as *"elegant, superb and airy"*. These words suggest that it was on the first floor, lit by the five tall windows which face down Great Pulteney Street, and the delay in completing it points again to the financial difficulties under which this whole scheme began.

The illustration on page 33 shows the garden front of the Tavern building. Visitors would enter from the street into the dark hall and look through to the far door to see the transparency, a picture painted on thin linen so that it glowed against the light. Projecting from the building at first-floor level is a greenhouse or conservatory, perhaps containing exotic arrivals from abroad like camellias, believed in the early 19th century to be too tender to resist the winter outside. The half-circle of the Orchestra platform projects from the Conservatory, creating a wide covered loggia underneath.

The rooms could all be hired for private parties and meetings. For example, the completion of the Somersetshire Coal Canal in April 1805 was celebrated with a dinner and a ball at Sydney House, after a jolly party of ladies and gentlemen, *"...attended by the Bath Forum Band, proceeded by water from Timsbury Bason through all the 22 locks at Combhay"*,

**A Wheel Chair**

A Light Park Chair, with cane or panelled body, made by Heath's Manufactory, Bath.

Katherine Plymley mentions that her mother, in 1803, was carried to Sydney Gardens in a sedan chair, and then *"taken round the gardens in a wheeling chair"*.[23]

It is likely that wheel chairs were kept for hiring out.

and thence along the Kennet and Avon Canal to Sydney Gardens. In May the same year, the Bath Harmonic Society hired the Banqueting Room to give an end-of-season party, which they called a *Fête Champêtre*. In the Gardens were four separate bands of music, presumably out of earshot of each other, to which the guests danced away the early summer day. The various garden buildings, including the Orchestra and Dining Boxes, were "*...converted into bowers of laurel, ... and loaded with most delicious oranges*". Sydney Gardens and its Tavern became, in fact, a venue for many local events, such as meetings of the Bath Volunteer Infantry, who "*... assembled ... and went through their different evolutions with great precision and exactness*", in June 1801. Their drill would have taken place on the wide area in front of the Tavern, with the orders being shouted from the vantage point of the Balcony. This arrangement made a good setting for meetings, and in 1831 a large gathering met here to be addressed on the Parliamentary Reform Bill. As the crowd, estimated by Mainwaring at 20,000 people, dispersed down Great Pulteney Street, bands playing, banners furling, they made a magnificent sight, "*... the music falling fainter on the ear as the dark multitude lessened in the distance*".[11]

In 1832 the ceremony of beating the bounds of the parish of Bathwick began at Sydney Hotel, and after perambulating to the western boundary at the exact mid-point of Pulteney Bridge and then climbing up to the eastern extremity at Sham Castle, the procession returned to Sydney House for "*a dinner in the most excellent style*".

# A Typical Early Gala

The Gala attended by Jane Austen on 4th June 1799 was spoilt by rain, so she went to the repeat performance two weeks later. The doors opened at 5.00, when the usual menu of cold ham, chicken, beef, lamb and tongue was available, with wine, spirits, bottled porter, cider and perry, all "*... as reasonable as possible, the prices of which will be affixed on the bills of fare, and placed in every conspicuous part of the garden*".

Over-charging by waiters was thus prevented. On a chilly evening there would be a temptation to eat inside, in the brand new Banqueting Room, and perhaps miss the start of the concert, which began at 7.00. Those eating in the out-door boxes or cubicles would have the option of staying there for the whole evening. The boxes made, in fact, a good vantage point for young blades wishing to inspect different categories of lady, as all arrivals passed in front of them.

As darkness gathered, thousands of lamps would be lit. Piers Egan writes,
> "*The gradual ascent of the principal walk, ... upon a gala night has a most brilliant effect, from the numerous variegated lamps with which it is ornamented ... The view, when seated in the* [stone] *pavilion, down to the orchestra, across arches covered with lamps, gives it a very captivating appearance.*"[12]

John Kerr is moved to greater rhapsody,

> *"In a dark night these illuminations are very beautiful and cannot fail to surprise and delight every susceptible spectator; but in a moonlight night there is something more peculiarly pleasing, which so strongly affects the imagination, that it instills an idea of enchantment."*[13]

### Jane Austen's Gala

The announcement of the gala on 18th June 1799, which Jane Austen attended. Note the name of Mr. Herschell among the orchestral players; this is Alexander, brother of the astronomer William.

There were three Galas each summer at this early period; the birthdays of George III on 4th June and the Prince of Wales on 12th August being the main excuses, with a more variable date in July to coincide with the Bath Races. In practice bad weather often led to repeat performances a few days later, as happened with this one. The year before, the tenant had expressed his regret at having to charge two shillings, and said he intended to hold future Galas without a concert, when the charge would be only one shilling.

*Sydney-Garden Vauxhall, Bath.*

The Disappointment experienced by a great number of Ladies and Gentlemen, on his Majesty's Birth-Day on account of the badness of the weather; and the repeated applications which T. Holloway, daily received from numerous Parties, induce him to announce so: EARLY PUBLIC NIGHT; he therefore respectfully solicits the patronage and attention of the Nobility and Gentry for TUESDAY next the 18th of JUNE, when as Brilliant ILLUMINATIONS, Superb FIRE-WORKS, and as FULL a CONCERT of MUSIC, Vocal and Instrumental, as were prepared to celebrate the King's Birth-Day, will be exhibited.

ON TUESDAY next the 18th of JUNE,
THERE WILL BE
A. GRAND GALA,
*In a Stile of Magnificence never exceeded.*
The Evening's Entertainment will consist of a
*Concert of Vocal & Instrumental Music,*
IN THE NEW ORCHESTRA;
In the course of which will be given,
THE WONDERFUL IMITATIONS OF BIRDS,
By ROSSIGNOL, Jun. viz.
The Black-Bird, Canary, Thrush, Sky-Lark Titter-Wren, Nightingale, and a variety of other Birds.
*Principal Vocal Performers,*

| Mr. Taylor, | Miss Tebay, |
| Mr. Shepherd, | Miss Richardson. |

*Principal Instrumental Performers,*
Leader of the Band, Mr. Richards; Violoncello, Mr. Herschell; Oboe, Mr. Ashley.
Act I. Overture, Haydn. Song, Mr. Shepherd. Glee. Song, Miss Richardson. Glee, *If delight.* Song, Miss Tebay. Song, Mr. Taylor.
Act II. Overture, Pleyel. Song, Miss Tebay. Glee, *Tutty Dutton.* Comic Song, Mr. Taylor. Glee. Song, Miss Richardson, Nightingale. Duet, Messrs. Cook and Taylor. Full Piece.
Act III. Overture, Haydn. Mr. Rossignol's Imitations. Comic Song, Mr. Taylor. Glee, *Genius of Liberty.* Finale.
Between the 2d and 3d Acts of the Concert,
THERE WILL BE A MOST
CAPITAL DISPLAY OF FIRE-WORKS
By Signor INVETTO,
Who will exert the utmost of his ingenious skill to produce new and astonishing effects; to enumerate the particulars would be too long for an advertisement.
The ILLUMINATIONS will be most BRILLIANT, several new Devices and Decorations.
*Private Parties will accommodated, in the New Banquet-ing Room, which, with other Rooms will be open for that purpose, and sufficient attendants engaged.*
Doors to be open at 5, and the Concert to begin at 7.
Tickets 2s. each, to be had at the Gate of the Garden. If the principal Inns, Libraries, and Music-shops, which it is requested, the Company will provide themselves with to prevent confusion at the entrance.
☞ The LAST PUBLIC BREAKFAST, at this Garden will be on MONDAY next.  1342

The Castle Ruin may also have been spookily illuminated for special Galas, while most of the narrow winding paths would remain enticingly shadowy. The raised Orchestra platform would be a blaze of light, and the Promenade area also, with lamps fixed to every pillar and festooned through the tree branches as well. The fireworks would have been prepared in advance by the Italian master, Invetto, and fixed to a wooden framework set up where indicated on the map on page 6 as "*space for fireworks*". The tradition owed much to theatrical scenery and assumed, in theory, a centrally-placed audience, as the display was symmetrically arranged. The frame was often built to look like a classical building, and called a Temple.

The cost to each visitor for five hours of summer evening entertainment was two shillings (£10 today). Jane Austen enjoyed the fireworks and illuminations, but deliberately avoided the concert by not arriving until 9.00. Beyond stating that the weather was favourable, which it had not been on the 4th, she gives us no information at all: no comment on the newly finished reception rooms in the Tavern, nor on the Orchestra, also new, nor on the garden itself.

**Announcement for a Gala at Sydney Gardens** a month after the one attended by Jane Austen, which gives a list of fireworks, similar to those she saw:

Maroons, from marrons, i.e. chestnuts which burst in the fire with a loud report. They are small boxes of flash powder covered with a paste of flame powder, so that they flare brilliantly before bursting.

Pots de Brin were rolls of paste board filled with basic gunpowder and a variety of stars, snakes, rains and crackers.

A pigeon was a small rocket propelled along a horizontal rope, sometimes used to ignite other pieces of the display.

Chinese Fire was gunpowder plus fine cast-iron filings, giving a more brilliant flame.

Serpents were small rockets without rods, which rose obliquely and descended in a zig-zag manner, which could be added to the charge inside a large rocket, so as to explode at the summit of its climb.[14]

Sky Rockets and a Fixed Sun can be seen in the artist's impression on page 34.

Sydney Garden Vauxhall, Bath.

ON TUESDAY next the 16th of July THERE WILL BE A GRAND GALA, In as superb a Stile as ever was attempted in this part of the Country.—With a Full

Concert of Vocal & Instrumental Music IN THREE ACTS.

Principal Vocal Performers,
Mr. TAYLOR, | Miss TERAY,
Mr. SHEPHERD, | Miss RICHARDSON
And Mrs. MATHER,
Being her first appearance here, and second in public.
Principal Instrumental Performers,
Leader of the Band, Mr. Richards, Violoncello, Mr
Herschell, Oboe, Ms. Ashley.
Between the 2d and 3d Acts of the Concert
THERE WILL BE A MOST
CAPITAL DISPLAY OF FIRE-WORKS
By Signor INVETTO.
Many Pieces entirely New —ORDER OF FIRING!
1. Battery of Maroons. 2. Six Sky-Rockets, ornamented with Stars. 3. Two Javelin Wheels of various motions. 4. A beautiful Sun-Flower Wheel, ornamented with various colours. 5. A Grand Piece called the Gillashears. 6. A beautiful Piece of Roman-Candles, with Wheel. 7. Two Pots de Brien. 8. Pigeon. 9. A grand Diamond Piece of Chinese Fire with a curious Wheel. 10. Beautiful Globe Illuminated. 11. A curious Fancy-Piece composed of Rain Fire, with a Wheel in the centre. 12. A Brilliant Sun fixed. 13. Six Rockets ornamented with Stars, Serpents, and Snakes. 14. A Bomb-shell illuminated.
The ILLUMINATIONS will be most BRILLIANT, with various new Devices and Decorations
Supper Parties well accommodated in the New Breakfast...other Spacious Rooms, which will b...

# The Canal

The first plan for the western end of the Kennet and Avon Canal, surveyed by John Rennie in 1793, shows it entering the Avon just below Bathampton Weir.[15] This would have avoided Sydney Gardens altogether, of course, but does not address the problem of how to get boats past Pulteney Weir in the centre of Bath. Some shareholders in the K&A company wanted the canal built directly to Bristol, and Rennie's second survey of 1796 takes the route as actually built, through Sydney Gardens, past Sydney Wharf, but with the arm from Widcombe second lock following roughly along the present A4 to Bristol. Funds were insufficient, however, and the Widcombe flight down to the site of Ralph Allen's old stone wharf became, in 1810, the terminating point of the K&A.

The price demanded by the Sydney Gardens committee for the disruption to their garden was 2,000 guineas, or £2,100, plus two cast-iron bridges for the Walks, and two ornamental stone bridges for the Ride. This much is documented, but we may be reasonably sure that the committee members, especially people like George Stothert senior and William Johnstone Pulteney himself, would have insisted on further details, such as keeping the canal in a 12-foot deep cutting so as to be out of sight of the elegant promenaders, and also to take a course which avoids the Castle ruin on one side, and the tip of the Labyrinth on the other. These landscape considerations were in fact turned to advantage by John Rennie, as after entering the gardens by one of the straight tunnels, the canal needs to turn through an angle of 20 degrees, which gave him the chance to make the centre pool wider than the others. This bulbous pool makes the course very sinuous, and, depending on where you stand, the canal almost turns into a Capability Brown lake, even to the two ends being mysteriously hidden from view – for a pleasure garden, a most appropriate blend of practicality and fantasy.

The landscape garden illusion is helped by the white-painted, cast-iron bridges, which were made in sections in the foundries of Colebrookdale and bolted together on site, quite new technology in 1800. They were first described as *"Chinese"* in the *New Bath Guide* the following year, because the rails, designed in squares and diagonals, are like the rails and fences in Chinoiserie decoration, as opposed to plain vertical bars. There is more fantasy on the stone portals, which show Old Father Thames and Sabrina, goddess of the Severn, respectively.

Reading between the lines, it seems likely that the digging of the canal section through Sydney Gardens began in the autumn of 1799 when the garden closed for the winter. Visitors in 1800 would have witnessed huge and muddy disruption, but no descriptions have come to light. The first recorded boat trip along this section took place on 10th June 1800, when K&A committee members travelled as far as the Monkton Combe aqueduct, after a meeting at Sydney House. Again reading between the lines, the completion of details like the stone-work and reconstruction of the garden near the canal, took a little longer, as it is not until March 1801 that the tenant includes it in his opening announcement for the new season:

*"The novelty of the Kennet & Avon Canal which is carried through the Garden and Ride, and completed in the most handsome manner, with Ornamental Iron Bridges, and with improvements in the plantations add considerably to the Picturesque Beauties for which this spot has been so universally admired."*

And so the first intrusion of transport technology into the elegant pleasure gardens was successfully accommodated. The official line continued to be that the delightful scene was a happy accident, resulting from the unexpectedly deep cutting that turned out to be necessary. Both Nattes[16], and Piers Egan[12], repeat this story. But today it should be obvious that the brilliant skill of John Rennie is what actually brought it about.[17]

---

**Music at Sydney Gardens**

The Pandean Band first performed in Sydney Gardens at a Grand Gala on 24th September 1812, the last Gala of John Gale's tenancy, having been *"expressly engaged at a very great expense, for the occasion"*. They are shown in this drawing by Edward Burney, playing five sizes of Pan Pipes, which are wedged inside their waistcoat collars. This leaves their hands free to play various percussion instruments, including a Turkish Crescent or 'Jingling Johnny', and a drum played with drum-stick and switch of twigs simultaneously.

Apart from occasional orchestral concerts, the music at this period was provided by small militia bands or a quartet of horns and clarinets, so the Pandeans were an exotic innovation. Their uniforms were splendid, and the combination of ethereal Pan Pipes with loud, jangling Turkish percussion, must have produced a very electrifying sound.

---

# Late Regency Developments

Sydney Gardens had opened as a late 18th-century garden, full of winding paths, glades, shrubberies and nicely contrived alcoves for drinking tea, its main purpose being the provision of an elegant meeting-place for the affluent classes. The possibilities for experiencing shivers of fear or excitement were limited to two – getting lost in the Labyrinth, or contemplating the Castle ruin and allowing one's imagination to dwell either on the melancholy effects of time and decay on the stoutest works of man, or, during an evening Gala, on Gothic horrors, as owls and bats swooped out of the shrouding ivy in the moonlight.

But as the 19th century passed its first quarter mark, such things were no longer exciting enough and the garden begins to fill up with gimmicks and titillations: frequent re-enactments of recent military victories done in fireworks, sometimes with the castle being the focus of a 'bombardment', or the visit of Siamese twins in 1830, to walk about and be stared at, to name two particularly extreme examples. All due, of course, to the onward march of the times, just as much as the intellectual curiosity which led to lectures being held in the Tavern's rooms, like a demonstration of fire-proof asbestos clothing in May 1830, and electro-magnetism in July 1834. There was also great interest in hot-air balloons, which made regular ascents from the Gardens.

In most cases we do not know the dates of new attractions in Sydney Gardens, but one exception is **The Cascade**, a rather strange spectacle first announced in May 1810.

> *"... for the first time will be exhibited, a very large & ornamental piece of Scenery & Machinery, prepared at a very great expense, representing a Beautiful Perspective View of a Village and Grand Cascade, a Water Mill at work, a Bridge with various Passengers, &c. &c."*

It was an artificial rural scene, like stage scenery, where the 'water' rushed down a ravine and the horses, carts and villagers moved across the bridge, all worked by a clockwork mechanism. It had to be wound up, and when it was demonstrated at an evening Gala, a bell would be rung to summon visitors to the spot, where they gazed in wonder for a few minutes, until the works ran down. Visitors' comments on the Cascade at the London Vauxhall show their fascination with the life-like effect:

> *"The exact appearance of water is seen, flowing down a declivity and, turning the wheel of the mill, it rises up in a foam at the bottom, and then glides away."*[18]

The 'water' was actually made from shreds of tin, which not only looked, but sounded like real water. Some who saw it, however, chose not to be persuaded. Leading style-journals, such as *The Connoisseur,* treated it with derision, and Smollet's Matthew Bramble, who is determined not to enjoy anything at Vauxhall, calls it *"a puppet-show representation of a tin cascade".*[19]

Both Sydney Gardens and Vauxhall Gardens got rid of their Cascades in the early 1820s, and both built open-air theatres instead.[20] In Bath the Theatre was used for rope-climbing and acrobatic acts.

**The Theatre** had, "*... a proscenium forming a bower, with a neatly painted frontispiece representing a picturesque flower garden, a romantic landscape with waterfall, whilst the numerous animated figures give an agreeable and effective relief to the picture, which is well illuminated by concealed lights.*"[13]

It had been painted by "*an eminent artist*", the current tenant informs us. This is a reminder of the important part played by painted effects in a Pleasure Garden. At Vauxhall Gardens these were provided by the likes of Hogarth and Francis Hayman, in a style which was by no means gaudy fairground, nor yet quaintly naive, but top quality representational painting.[21] At Sydney Gardens the dining boxes did not have painted scenes, as at Vauxhall, but the rooms inside the Tavern are likely to have been decorated, as were other structures, including the Tea House, later called the Middle Bar;[22] a *trompe-l'oeil* archway described by one visitor in 1803;[23] and numerous transparencies also.

**Madame Saqui**, "*the celebrated performer on the rope at Vauxhall*", pictured in *La Belle Assemblée* magazine in 1820. Wroth quotes a description of her as "*... a lady of muscular and masculine appearance bedecked with spangles and waving plumes*".[24] The trapeze artist ascended a 350-foot long inclined rope fixed to a mast 60 feet high, looking almost supernatural amid a glare of blue flame. She then descended again, through a shower of chinese fire, and "*... in the face of a tempest of fireworks*".

Similar artists were seen at Sydney Gardens from 1820 onwards. The rope would be stretched from the roof of the Tavern to the ground, and on it Il Diavolo Antonio performed "*feats of agility*". In 1828 a Monsieur Lalanne ascended this rope pushing a wheel-barrow. He and his wife also gave dancing displays together on a horizontal rope.

**The Aviary** was introduced in 1824, when the last three dining boxes on the north side were converted, in order to house

> "... *a variety of the most rare and valuable feathered species, whose melody, in unison with the numerous tribe who have established their residence in the Gardens, forms one of Nature's most pleasing and happiest concerts.*"[13]

The cages were unfortunately burgled four years later, when, out of a population of about 140 birds, "*in fine plumage and full song*", between 80 and 100 were stolen, along with some eggs and some of the equipment. The birds were "*... of considerable value, and had been carefully kept with stoves to warm their habitation in the winter*".[25]

Exactly opposite the Aviary, a **Cosmorama** was made out of the last three dining boxes on the south side. This was an indoor peepshow, where paintings of distant places such as dramatic scenes in the Alps, a panorama of Florence, or Vesuvius in the act of erupting, were brightly lit, and when seen through convex glass windows, they would appear life-size. The Cosmorama was a French invention, which reached London in 1821, and must have come to Sydney Gardens by 1824.

Just below the Cosmorama, on the edge of the Garden, "*at the extremity of a rising walk*", stood the **Hermit's Cot**, (i.e. cottage). The Hermit, a robed puppet figure, sat in his open-sided, roughly constructed hut, its walls hung with strange mystic symbols, "*quietly perusing his homilies*". A transparent painting of coals in his grate glowed at night, and no doubt there was also a guttering candle or two. The aim was to give the impression that the recluse lived miles from anywhere without human contacts, and his purpose, in a pleasure garden, was to darken the mood momentarily.[13] It would also have had snobbish allusions, as some Sydney Gardens visitors, at least, will have known that Queen Charlotte's 1790's picturesque garden at Frogmore near Windsor Castle contained a hermit's cell.

**The Watermill** or Miller's Habitation was again made of painted scenery, and like the Hermit's Cot and the Cosmorama scenes was the work of the same "*eminent artist*". It was powered by water from one of the natural springs in the upper part of the garden, which turned a real water-wheel. A stream ran off from the Castle moat down the hillside, possibly in an underground conduit, and surfaced again to create two water features. The first was a pond, and lower down on the edge of the north Bowling Green there was a waterfall. The higher pond is the most likely site for the Watermill, but its date is not known.

A map which illustrates the Gardens at this period is that by John Pinch the younger, shown on the next page.

The opening of Victoria Park in Bath in October 1830 signalled not so much an immediate threat to Sydney Gardens, as a foretaste of the future. It was a good dozen years ahead of the "*parks for the people*" movement of the later 19th century, but marked the beginning of the end for the notion of a green open space which cost money to enter and enjoy. Sydney Gardens had many advantages over Victoria Park,

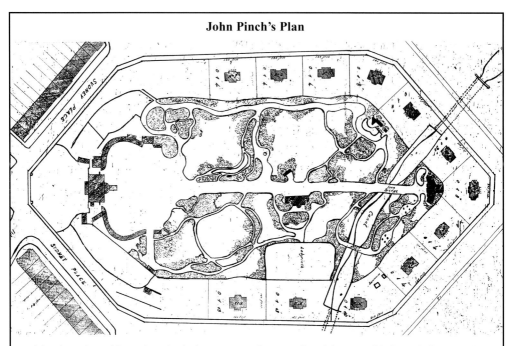

This plan, signed by John Pinch the younger, but not dated, is most likely to belong to the period around 1830 when similar proposals were made for detached villas elsewhere in Bath, but before the route of the railway through Sydney Gardens was known, in 1833 or so. The villa scheme was not carried out; but this plan gives valuable detail which is not found again before the Ordnance Survey maps in the mid 1880s.

Beginning at the western (left) end, Harcourt Masters' tavern is shown, with small buildings to the north of the forecourt which would be stables and coach-houses, and to the south the Sydney Tap, a public house for the use of servants. All these are concealed behind the curved screen walls so as not to upset the visual scheme. The Sydney Tap was not in the basement, as often stated; this would have involved mere coachmen entering by the same door as their employers. It was a separate building and let to a sub-tenant.[26]

On the garden side is the projecting orchestra, and the dining boxes in two curves. At the north end are the Aviary and the Theatre, at the south the Cosmorama, and on the edge at the end of a straight walk, the Hermit's Cot. Half-way along the main Walk is an alcove, and opposite, the Middle Bar, formerly the Chinese Tea House. At the north corner is the Castle Ruin, and at the extreme end of the Walk, the stone pavilion or Loggia.

The exact lay-out of the small winding paths and areas of shrubbery can be seen, hardly changed from the original design of 1795. Water features are, disappointingly, not shown, except for the Castle moat.

however, in its position, its exclusive atmosphere, and above all, in the charm of the garden itself, by now maturing into a thickly-planted woodland. An advertisement of 1824 describes it as

"... *tastefully laid out in shrubbery, lawns, Bowling Green, public and retired Walks, with a well-arranged Labyrinth, Orchestra, Alcoves and other Ornamental Buildings. The trees, shrubs and plants are in the greatest perfection and the whole forms one of the most delightful and luxuriant Public Gardens in Britain.*"

A typical Gala of this period was held on 26th June 1834, when the tenant, Mr Chatterton, invited the entire troupe of performers from London's Vauxhall Garden to travel to Bath with their illuminations and fireworks. The programme, which takes up a newspaper column 20 inches long, included,

- A vocal and instrumental Concert, with six singers; the band led by Bianchi Taylor, who in spite of his name was a Bathonian.

- Illuminated Tableau of the Bath City Arms, and of the Royal Garter, having '*Honi Soit qui Mal y Pense*' in golden lamps, entwined with evergreen branches.

- The Court Band of the Grand Duke of Hesse Darmstadt, "*his Serene Highness having kindly consented that they might quit Germany for six weeks, to perform for the Vauxhall Proprietors only*".

- A Comic Scene entitled Shades in the Moon, or The Magic Circle.

- An immense firework display totalling 32 items. No. 8 is "*A Shell, with bright stars, forming a tree in full blossom*". No.15 is "*The much admired Fiery Dragon: this curious piece will propel itself over the heads of the spectators to and fro several times, displaying various fires*". No.23 is "*A large Shell, throwing out a nest of snakes, at a great elevation*".

- At the end, A Fire Balloon, "*of large dimensions, will be despatched into the air, and at great altitude will explode, and emit various coloured fire*".

Admission to the gala was 2s.6d., which represents only a 25% increase on the 1799 price paid by Jane Austen.

In addition, the Gardens now became the setting for a new kind of summer event: sumptuous flower shows, with marquees full of elaborate displays, a band playing all afternoon, and such large numbers of visitors that they got in each others' way when trying to inspect the exhibits.

**A Balloon Ascent from Vauxhall Gardens in 1849**

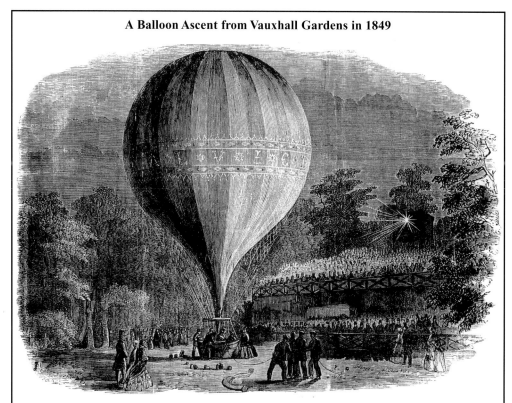

The first balloon flight from Sydney Gardens was in September 1802, when the Frenchman André Garnerin, who was touring England with his balloon and his entourage, visited Bath immediately after an appearance at Vauxhall Gardens. High prices were charged to view the balloon being filled: 5 shillings, and double this for the advantage of a seat on the orchestra platform. The balloon was then towed, "*at a slight elevation*", along the walk and back to the Promenade area, to give spectators a good view of it. It then took off, at the mercy of the elements, and reached Mells Park, near Frome, on this occasion. *(Picture by courtesy of the Guildhall Library, London)*

# The Bath Horticultural & Floral Society

The society was formed in 1834 by landowners and wealthy citizens with the object of "*... encouraging floral and horticultural productions, and to give the labouring man some inducement to employ his leisure hours usefully and rationally*". Sydney Gardens was the natural choice of venue for the new Society's five annual shows, being completely walled and fenced, and having only one entrance, in addition to its being a "*beautiful sylvan setting*".

Several of its committee members were also officers of the new Society, but the latter still paid a fee to the Sydney Gardens tenant for the use of the grounds.

Judging by the reports of the Shows in the local papers over the following 20 years, with their glowing descriptions of the flower displays, and long lists of prize winners, the aims of the Society were amply realised. While the working man duly brought along his apples, potatoes and turnips with nosegays of flowers according to season, to compete in his own "*Cottager's*" class, the gentry with their spacious grounds, hot and cold glass houses and numerous gardeners to do the hard work, showed the latest imported tropical plants sent home by the plant hunters, as well as strawberries in May, and pineapples and grapes in all the Shows from May to September. The rather dry business of listing each and every prize-winner five times a year is not shirked, but the journalists also convey their admiration for the plants brought along simply to be exhibited, and no doubt discussed and compared by their owners and by the head gardeners who had grown them.

To take examples from just the first three years of Shows; the Spring events had a class for hyacinths, which specifies the beautiful double form, in red, blue, white, and yellow, now sadly almost extinct, "*... no flower to take a prize unless it has 12 bells in bloom and the stem not supported*".

Azaleas, the new fashion, were brought in large numbers from Exeter by the firm of Luccombe, to produce a dazzling display, and one of the garden buildings was decorated entirely with wild flowers from the Bath district:

> "*... every pillar was wreathed with the indigenous wild flowers of the neighbour-hood which were also disposed in wreaths, festoons and bouquets around the exterior and on the centre table ... It was computed that a million cowslips, blue and white hyacinths (i.e. bluebells), violets and primroses, and 700 thousand of such varieties of the orchis, and other plants as are not commonly met with in profusion, were used.*"

The Summer Shows required four tents, plus the curved Loggia, the disused dining boxes, and outdoor space as well, to accommodate all the flowers, fruit and vegetables. The large marquee presented

> "*... a gorgeous* coup d'oeil *from the immense collection of plants of every imaginable tint ... The centre pavilion on the right of the promenade was completely filled with a grand collection of orange and citron trees in full bearing.*"

In July 1836 someone had succeeded in producing "*... a splendid double yellow moss rose in full bloom*". There was a figure of Flora in her bower,

> "*... composed of thousands of roses, her features of rose leaves, her eyes and eyebrows of pansies, her turban of roses and evergreens, her neckchain of yellow ranunculus and the drops in her ears of hemerocallis or day-lily ...*"

To the next Show the firm of Salter on the London Road brought 380 potted plants, this number not including their displays of cut flowers.

The early Autumn Shows were the province of dahlias, just becoming popular, the first competitive class being for no less than 50 blooms of different sorts. The sign 'FLORA' in letters four feet high greeted the visitors, formed of more than 2,000 dahlia flowers. To another September Show, J. Phelps Esq. of Warminster brought,

> *"... the most strikingly curious and beautiful plant, a most stately specimen, 12 feet high, of Gloriosa Superba* [the Glory Lily]. *It arrived too late for competition owing to the difficulty of transmitting it uninjured."*

Mr. Phelps had driven with this prodigy in his own carriage, in an effort to get it to Sydney Gardens unharmed.

The correspondent of the Chronicle sums up the general feeling:

> *"To the unwearied labours of the Hon. Secretary and Committee, the public of Bath are indebted for one of the most agreeable and rational enjoyments and recreations of the whole season."*

Although he is writing specifically of the fourth Show in 1835, he could be summing up for us the whole of this happy period, which seems with hindsight like a final flowering of the old, unaltered Sydney Gardens.

# The Hotel Expands

1836 was the year when utilitarian additions to Sydney Gardens began in earnest. An extra floor of bedrooms was built on top of the Hotel, raising the roof line even higher. The tenant in charge had announced two years before, that he would change the Tavern into a *"Private Lodging House"*, and would leave only the Coffee Room for the use of Pleasure Garden visitors. It was evidently becoming more difficult to make a respectable profit each season from the Gardens alone.

It seems reasonable to assume that Sydney House, at the upper end of the main Walk and facing onto Warminster Road, was built at the same time as the extra bedrooms, and by the same architect, John Pinch the younger. The evidence for this claim is that the new villa is listed as *"Sydney House"* in the Bath Directories from 1837, while the Tavern is re-named *The Pulteney Hotel*, to avoid confusion.

I would suggest also, that the curved Loggia, seen in Wise's drawing, on page 35, was rebuilt at the same time, on the same foundations, but in a less fragile form, so as to make a satisfactory composition with the new villa (see opposite). Pinch has minimised the cliff-like impact of the three-storey villa on the Gardens, by having a stepped arrangement of the upper floors, and a semi-circular first-floor drawing room which echoes the shape of the Loggia beneath.

All these changes, while made for good economic reasons at the time, are inevitably seen today as beginning to destroy the purity of the original design. The greatest damage from this point of view was done by the cutting for the Great Western Railway, which divided the garden lay-out into two forlorn halves.

**A View of the Main Walk in Sydney Gardens**

An undated etching by Hollway showing the scene which would have greeted visitors as they emerged from the back of the Hotel or Tavern into the gardens. The vista is the more dramatic for the funnel effect of the maturing trees. At the summit of the Walk stands not only the Loggia, which had been there from the start, but Sydney House, built in sympathetic style immediately behind it, which suggests that this scene was drawn to commemorate its building. No railway bridge is visible, so the date must be before 1839. The ladies' costumes have lost the huge gathered sleeves of the years just before Victoria's accession in 1837.

The tree to the right with a firework device attached, and people sitting on a circular seat, is possibly the large London Plane still standing at the edge of what is now the Holburne Museum garden. Its companion to the left is no longer there.

Note the long rustic bench just behind this tree; also the Aviary, extreme left, with a large parrot on a perch.

**The Loggia**

**The Pavilion**, as it was, by G.M. Brodribb, 1936. This is the second of two surviving drawings of the Loggia, made only 60 years ago. It shows a building with several differences from the one drawn by George Wise c.1810 (see p.35). It has paired columns resting on piers; it has double pilasters in place of the exquisite but probably fragile corners mid-way along the concave curves; it has solid end walls with arches cut out; the cherubs on the roof are wide apart and the shield between them has gone. So, if the Loggia drawn by Wise was the original of 1795, presumably designed by Thomas Baldwin, this one,

drawn by Brodribb, seems similar but more robust. This suggests that the first one became unsafe and was rebuilt, 'to last', while retaining some of the charm of the original. Logic would also suggest that the villa behind and attached to it, was designed to harmonise, and was built at the same time. This would mean a date of 1836, making it exactly 100 years old when Brodribb drew it; only just in the nick of time, as it was demolished two years later.

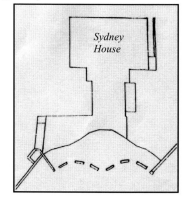

Sydney House

**The Loggia**, as rebuilt c.1836, is accurately shown on Cotterel's 1852/54 map of Bath (*right*). The sharp corners along the concave front which distinguish Wise's version, and which appear on Harcourt Masters' 1795 map, are no longer there.

# The Railway

In 1799 the canal had been planned so as to avoid two of the important structures in the Gardens. No such nicety hindered the imperious sweep of Isambard Kingdom Brunel's Great Western, the epic masterpiece of technology which was going to provide cheap travel for the multitudes. Brunel faced tricky problems either side of Sydney Gardens, with houses to the south, and the canal plus land sloping down to the river, on the north. A plan of 1837 shows the line passing between Hampton Row and the river, implying a deeper cutting, and there is evidence that the Sydney Gardens stretch was going to be roofed-in. But this line curved too sharply, and Brunel's solution was to go south of Hampton Row, even though this required a re-alignment of the canal for a short distance.

It is hard to discover exactly when the works through the gardens were begun, in the face of an apparent watertight resolve by the GWR in its adverts for tenders, and Brunel in his half-yearly reports to shareholders, never to mention Sydney Gardens by name. By December 1839 the works north and south of the gardens were well advanced, so probably the deep gash had been excavated by then. Some idea of the damage done is gained by comparing the maps on pages 24 and 46. The whole of the Tea House or Middle Bar was swept away, along with the west half of the Labyrinth and most of the Castle. Two bridges were built to connect the footpaths, the main Walk having a skew bridge to preserve its axial straight line, as had been provided over the canal in 1800. The paths west of the Castle were severed, so that the last remains of a perimeter walk around the garden, possible in 1795, were now destroyed.

The finished cutting gives a certain dignity to the gardens. The impressive retaining wall with viewing terrace, the ornamental balustrade and the two bridges are in sober classical style, Brunel having wisely decided to fit the railway to the timeless architecture of the Hotel building, rather than launch into the jokiness of Jacobean or Medieval fantasy, as he did at other places on the Great Western.

The very first train to steam through Sydney Gardens was a trial run in the early hours of 30th June 1841, when an engine bearing Brunel, accompanied by a government safety inspector, left Paddington at 3.00am. It tested the whole line to Bristol, in spite of the fact that the GWR had been operating passenger trains since 1838 as far as Maidenhead, and between Bath and Bristol since 1840. The Chippenham to Bath section, where Sydney Gardens lies, was the last to open, having been held up by the difficulties of the Box Tunnel works. When the railway is at last mentioned in newspaper reports of the Flower Shows, the response is the same as with the canal 40 years before.

> "*The cutting of the railroad through the upper part of the grounds which it was at first supposed would materially injure their appearance has had the opposite effect. ... a beautiful stone parapet ... was crowded with different groups of spectators ... who watched with pleasurable anxiety the passing of the trains.*"

Another 16 years are to pass before any sense of regret is voiced for what might have been lost by allowing such an invasion.

**The railway cutting through Sydney Gardens**; one of the illustrations from J.C. Bourne's *The Great Western Railway*, published in 1846. This dramatic viewpoint gives a perspective through three bridges and a tunnel, about half a mile before Bath Station. Brunel's system had no transverse sleepers. The first train through Sydney Gardens, on 30th June 1841, was followed by a two-hourly service from Paddington which reached Bath 3³/₄ hours later.

*Right, above*: **The Garden Front of the Tavern**, drawn by John Nattes in 1805. This charming aquatint shows a daytime event in Sydney Gardens, most probably a Public Breakfast. People are eating in the dining boxes, and the band has evidently just left its platform for a refreshment break. Note the transparency in the arch, and the large windows of the first floor conservatory.

*Right, below*: **Camellias**, from left to right:
◆ Camellia sasanqua from China; illustration in *Curtis's Botanical Magazine*, Vol.46, 1819.
◆ A red camellia, name unknown, growing in the conservatory at Chiswick House, London. This conservatory was specially built to grow camellias in 1813, and the plants now blooming there are thought to be the original specimens.
◆ Camellia alba plena, introduced to Britain in 1792, which also grows at Chiswick; illustration from *Nouvelle Iconographie des Camellias*, by Gand, 1849.
*(Royal Horticultural Society, Lindley Library)*

An Artist's Impression of the Sydney Gardens Fireworks. (*Juliet Greaves*)

The gardens of Vauxhall, London, on a Gala evening, about 1810.

**The Two Chinese Bridges.** *(top)* A view of the Canal looking north, George Wise of Tonbridge, c.1810. Seen here from the towpath, the canal winds out of sight like a sinuous lake in a landscape garden. Note the loggia, above right: this is the only drawing of the original building which survives. Today the canal, bridge and tunnel are unchanged, while the Loggia has been rebuilt and is overshadowed by the large house behind.

*(right)* A close-up view of the **south canal bridge**. The cast-iron sections were made in Coalbrookdale and assembled on site, probably in June 1800. The first boat trip was made at the same time, as far as the Dundas Aqueduct at Monkton Combe. The top railing was added to the original *chinoiserie* design in 1992.

## Flowers from the Early Horticultural Shows

(*top*): Azaleas; examples of some of the native species from India, imported in the early 19th century. By the time of the Sydney Gardens shows in the mid-1830s, these azaleas had spread among nurseries and amateur enthusiasts, and were being extensively hybridised. Hand-coloured engravings from *Curtis's Botanical Magazine*, 1812-1826.

(*bottom left*): A group of double hyacinths, illustrated in Robert Thornton's *The Temple of Flora*, 1812. (*Royal Horticultural Society, Lindley Library*)

(*bottom right*): The Glory Lily, Gloriosa superba. A prodigious specimen of this East African plant, 12 feet in height, was grown by a keen plantsman of Warminster and brought to the Sydney Gardens show in September 1836. Hand-coloured engraving from *Curtis's Botanical Magazine*, 1825.

The Fern-Leaf Beech (*left*), was 88 feet high and "*a fine, domed tree*", when seen by Alan Mitchell[27]. By 1994 it had become lop-sided after losing several limbs in successive winter gales, and although healthy, in its prime in fact, it was reluctantly felled and a young specimen planted in its place.

**Two beech trees** in the present Holburne Museum grounds, which may have been planted about 1863 or 1864, to mark the 10th anniversary of the Proprietary College which held the tenancy at that time.

The Weeping Beech (*below*), seems to be a survivor of the shrubbery which used to frame the entrance court, the date of which is not known, but which is shown on the plan on page 46. There are no other ornamental beeches in Sydney Gardens apart from recent plantings. This supports the idea that the Proprietary College undertook some planting of its own in the Gardens, using these two comparatively uncommon varieties of beech tree, which had been first introduced, incidentally, in the 1830s.

**Roses**

Four roses which featured in the National Rose Society Show held at Sydney Gardens on 28th June 1882. (*from left to right*): Marechal Neil, Baroness Rothschild, Marie van Houtte, Louis van Houtte, taken from William Paul's *The Rose Garden*, 9th edition, 1888. *(Royal Horticultural Society, Lindley Library)*

'**An Evening Scene in the Sydney Gardens**'. A painting of about 1900. *(Boodle Collection)*

**The Bathwick Street Pay-Box** *(below)*

Drawing by the architect, Alfred J. Taylor, MSA, signed by him in March 1914. The centre pane of glass on the bottom row opens for the sale of admission tickets. The pay-box still stands by the Bathwick Street Gate, but is no longer used.

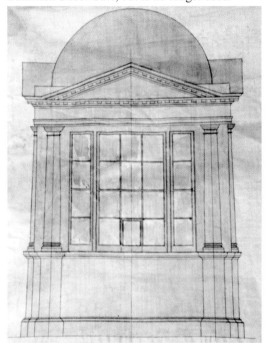

**The Temple of Minerva and the Catalpa Tree Today** *(above)*

Also known as the Indian Bean Tree, although it hails from south eastern U.S.A, Catalpa erubescens flowers from late July into August, and the long thin seed pods remain on the tree over winter. This hybrid form is rare. The Sydney Gardens tree is one of only three large examples named by Mitchell,[27] apart from a group in Surrey. Several more were victims of the 1987 gale. Another, missed by Mitchell, is in Bristol University grounds at The Holmes, Stoke Park Road, Bristol.

The leaf shape can be compared with that of the Southern Catalpa (C. bignonioides), *left*, a young tree standing to the north of the Holburne Museum. The Southern Catalpa was introduced in 1726, the hybrid in 1891.

**The Green Room**.  Three exhibits shown in the summer of 1995

The Bauhau Dessau, a 'billboard sculpture' by Langlands & Bell.

Fibre-glass heads telling the story of
Little Red Riding Hood,
by Diana Lorenzo Saxby.

The Croix Champêtre by Nigel Coates and Buro Happold *(left)*

All the structures except the billboard were vandalised during the four months of the exhibition.

An accompanying leaflet explained the thinking behind these, and further, structures, recalling the early 19th-century booklets, which were issued on Gala nights to help visitors to understand the subjects of the illuminations and transparencies, as well as printing the words of songs to be performed in the concert.

For the extra wide cutting we have to thank Brunel's 7ft $0^1/_4$in gauge, replaced by the modern 4ft $8^1/_2$in gauge in 1892. Another legacy is the track-side gravel path at the south end, evidently resulting from the removal of part of the hillside in order to make a level access road to bring in stone, rails and timber, and to take away numberless cart-loads of soil. The area was subsequently re-grassed, but the path is still in place.

The mature conifers here are typical Victorian random planting. They include a fine Irish Yew, a magnificent Atlas Cedar, a large and very fine Weeping Yew on the bank of the footbridge, a Deodar, and a Wellingtonia (Sequoiadendron giganteum). The latter, not having been introduced into Europe until 1853, indicates that the mess caused by the GWR works was not made good for at least a decade after the railway was completed.

**A Firefly class engine** emerging from one of Brunel's decorated tunnels between Bath and Bristol; the frontispiece of J.C.Bourne's *The Great Western Railway*. An engine of this class, for example a Firebrand, Fireking or Fireball, is likely to have been hauling the very first passenger train to pass through Sydney Gardens on 30th June, 1841. The Firefly was designed by the young Superintendent of Locomotives to the Great Western, Daniel Gooch. An eventual total of 62 were built, and all gave good service with minor modifications, until superseded by the narrow gauge locomotives in 1870.

## The Conifers

Three of the conifers near the railway, probably planted as a group, after the railway works were completed.

*from the left*:
Wellingtonia, which has a blunt tip, possibly caused by lightning, now regenerating;

Deodar Cedar; see also a young specimen on the lawn above the railway terrace;

Atlantic or Atlas Cedar, not the blue form which is more commonly seen.

The dates of introduction are:
Wellingtonia 1853, Deodar Cedar 1831 and Atlas Cedar 1841.

There were upheavals of another kind in 1839/40 when the original Horticultural Society had disagreements and split in two. One section formed a separate Society, and purchased its own garden in Victoria Park, where the Botanic Gardens now are. The Sydney Gardens Society quickly built an 'Octagonal Rustic Pavilion', seen on the map on page 46, as a 'refreshment room', which remained in place for 50 years. It was

> "... a light and elegant erection constructed of unbarked wood, in the form of an octagon and surmounted by a Lantern of similar shape."

It was 35 feet in diameter and could be approached on all eight of its sides. At the first flower Show of 1840, four of the doors were approached by corridors through temporary 'Venetian Tents', along the sides of which stages were placed for the floral exhibits.

The *Chronicle* correspondent also mentions an ornamental pool containing a seven-jet fountain, backed by an 'artificial rockery', on the east side of the pavilion. The site of this rockery is still present as a stone ledge beside the path leading from Minerva's Temple down to the Bowls Club green.

After two seasons of separate shows, the societies merged once again, and from 1842 the re-named Bath Royal United Horticultural Society held six shows annually, at Sydney Gardens and Victoria Park alternately, until 1853.

There is an advertisement for a 'Water Cure establishment' in October 1843, but it appears to be no more than an attempt to increase business for the Hotel in the off season, by offering the services of a physician who happened to live nearby in Great Pulteney Street. Few individuals seem to have been persuaded to try this mysterious treatment, for it was not advertised a second time. Clearly this was an unsettled period, when each new tenant tried something different, as it was becoming increasingly difficult to make the original concept of Hotel plus Pleasure Garden pay its way, although the three Flower Shows each summer were always a great success. By 1845 the Ball Room had been redecorated and named the 'Gothic Hall', and was used for orchestral concerts, theatrical entertainments, lectures, an indoor Chrysanthemum Show, and a dance at the August 1849 Gala.

# The Bath Proprietary College

In August 1853 the school of this name became the tenant of the Hotel and Gardens, and stayed until 1880 when it was amalgamated with Bath College. The committee must have been relieved to find a solution to their financial problems, but as the records of Sydney Gardens are lost, we do not know if they felt any sadness at bringing to an end what had become known as 'The Vauxhall of the West'. The London Vauxhall was subject to the same social change and financial difficulties, and closed down six years later in 1859. Sydney Gardens did survive, by moving with the times, and absorbing a good many compromises.

With the Hotel and grounds let, the committee added further to its income in 1853 by leasing out more land for building, and the two semi-detached houses on Sydney Road were constructed, at first name Lonsdale and Ravenswell. They occupy what had become a 'dead corner' between railway and canal, but their gardens extend beyond the old Ride and Meadow area, and this is land permanently lost to the park. While partly obscured by trees, their roof-lines are an inescapable item in the landscape on the south of Sydney Gardens, where the Italian exuberance of their Victorian 'Alpine Picturesque', places the scene irretrievably in the mid-19th century. The tall conifers add to this, especially the Wellingtonia which is more or less a trade mark of 1853.[28] Nowhere in Sydney Gardens is the original late 18th-century scene so fundamentally obliterated as here.

With the College installed as tenant, the Horticultural Shows had to go elsewhere, and when two of the 1854 shows had bad weather and another had greatly reduced competitive entries, disaster loomed. In January 1855 the debts were liquidated, and the B.R.U.H.S. was declared at an end.

# The Hanoverian Band Committee

Riding quickly to the rescue, however, were some Bath businessmen who supplied fresh thinking to the whole situation, and backed this up with their own cash. They first organised the summer open-air music for Bath in general, by engaging the Hanoverian Band to play *"twice daily at such times and places as may be thought most desirable"*; and

## PEACE HOLIDAY FETE,

### SYDNEY-GARDENS, Bath,

#### THURSDAY, 29th May, 1856.

The **HANOVERIAN BAND COMMITTEE** have the pleasure to announce that an arrangement has been made with the **Exhibitors of Flowers, Plants, &c.,** at the *FLORAL FETE,* to permit them to remain on **View** this Day.

*On this occasion the Plants will be Grouped as at the*

## CRYSTAL PALACE FETE.

IN ADDITION TO THE

## HANOVERIAN BAND,

(By the permission of COLONEL MILES, M.P.), the

## BAND OF THE NORTH SOMERSET YEOMANRY CAVALRY

### WILL ATTEND.

The **COMMITTEE**, anxious that all should enjoy this opportunity of Viewing the Beautiful Display of Horticultural Produce, and that the Return of **PEACE** may be celebrated in the most attractive and rational manner, have decided that the Admission to the **FETE** shall be

*From* 11 *to* 2 *o'Clock,* 1s. : 2 *to* 5 *o'Clock,* 6d.,

At which Hour the Gates will be closed.

NO SUBSCRIBERS' TICKETS-available at the PEACE HOLIDAY FETE.

*Money only taken, and the Public are requested to come provided with change.*

The Sydney-Gardens Committee and the Hanoverian Band Committee with much pleasure carry into effect a suggestion of the Mayor, by granting permission for all the Children in the several Charity Schools in the *City of Bath* to View the Show from 9 to 11 o'Clock.

MEYLER AND SON, PRINTERS, HERALD OFFICE, BATH.

**Bill to advertise a fete in Sydney Gardens**, celebrating the end of the Crimean War. (size 46 by 28 cm., from the Hunt Collection)

1856 was only the second year in which the Hanoverian Band Committee had taken on the running of summer out-door entertainments in Bath, following the disbanding of the Horticultural Society. Note that the time allotted to the lowest priced entry is now for three hours, instead of the former one: for example, in April 1853 entry had cost 2/6, at 4pm 1/-, and 3d. each for the working classes at 4.30pm.

The journalist remarks the next year, that horticulture is indeed classless, *"as roses display as much loveliness by a cottage as by a mansion"*. This democratic idea was so new that he expanded on it: *"In the present day, there is frequently more beauty within the wicket-gate of the husbandman's dwelling than existed in the stately gardens enclosed by the castle walls of our ancestors."*

they planned Horticultural Fetes, but only two per year. The Proprietary College's lease was altered so that they kept a much smaller area of garden, namely the original promenade between the two arms of dining boxes. They were probably happy to relinquish the rest of Sydney Gardens and be free of the upkeep expenses. But whether this revised arrangement was by their request or not, it gave the public-spirited businessmen the use of the Gardens once again, although without the former Hotel building.

The new committee proved to be good judges of what the public wanted, and in their first few years of Floral Fetes and daily Band Concerts, produced such a surplus of funds that they were able to make improvements to the Gardens, as well as to keep up the normal tidying and planting. They had understood the general drift of the times, and although the framework of the Shows was the same, with competitive exhibits judged by experts, the elitist atmosphere of the old landowner's fraternity had gone. Advertising was now aimed more widely, commercial plant growers from far afield were sending comprehensive displays, and by the second Fete, cheap railway excursions were run from surrounding towns specially for the Sydney Gardens Floral Fetes. Soon the Abbey bells were rung on the mornings of Fete days, and Bath shops were closing on Fete afternoons so that everyone could attend.

The changes made to the Gardens at this period are shown on the plan overleaf. All the alterations were practical, in order to improve the grounds for the management of large crowds. Thus the paths needed widening, and many small footpaths from the original layout were grassed over, trees and shrubs removed, and lawns extended, to accommodate the ever increasing size of the huge marquees. In 1866 the largest tent was 150 feet long, and christened *"The Queen of the West"*, and by 1874 the tent covering the Turf Banks had grown to 250 feet long. (The Floral Marquee at present-day Bath Spring Flower Shows is 300 feet long).

A bigger entrance was made at the south gate to the old Ride, and given an ironwork arch that was decorated with flowers on Show days. Just inside, a little stone hut with a small fireplace was built, *"for the convenience of the Gatekeeper in wet weather"*. The gate opposite New Sydney Place, with its wrought-iron lamp over-throw, was made to ease the exit of large crowds, and in 1861 came the splendid Orchestra, designed by local architect Charles Phipps. It was described by the Chronicle correspondent as,

> *"... a light and elegant structure, remarkably well adapted for sound, and in harmony with the lovely scenery of the gardens. The woodwork burnishing and the painted ornamentation of the interior have been well carried out, the colours having been artistically chosen ... Retiring rooms and stowage for chairs are provided in the rear, and altogether the building forms a feature that reflects credit on the judgement and enterprise of the managers."*

The main Walk had to be widened into a seating area, and, with the paling fence which now enclosed the College playground being screened from view by shrubs, planted that same year, the denial of the original axial lay-out became complete. The Victorians would surely have re-designed the entire path lay-out into curves and circles, like Henrietta Park (1897), had the railway not stood in their way.

# Changes During the Early Victorian Period

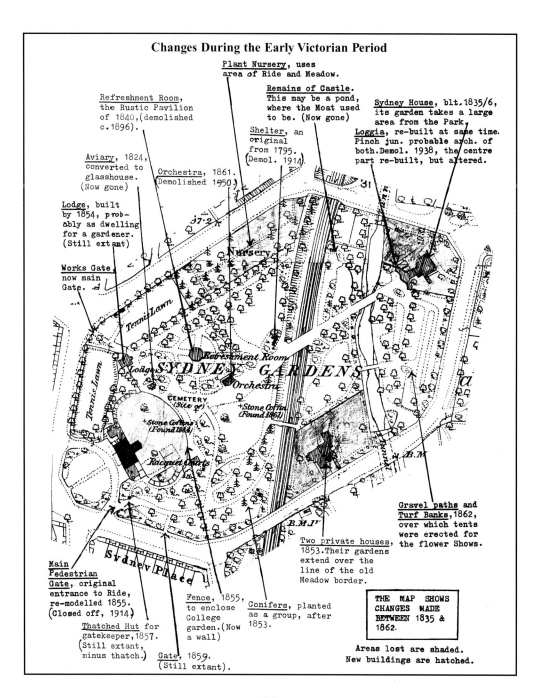

**Plant Nursery**, uses area of Ride and Meadow.

**Remains of Castle.** This may be a pond, where the Moat used to be. (Now gone)

**Refreshment Room**, the Rustic Pavilion of 1840,(demolished c.1896).

**Sydney House**, blt.1835/6, its garden takes a large area from the Park. **Loggia**, re-built at same time. Pinch jun. probable arch. of both.Demol. 1938, the centre part re-built, but altered.

**Shelter**, an original from 1795. (Demol. 1914).

**Aviary**, 1824, converted to glasshouse. (Now gone)

**Orchestra**, 1861. (Demolished 1950.)

**Lodge**, built by 1854, probably as dwelling for a gardener. (Still extant)

**Works Gate**, now main Gate.

**Main Pedestrian Gate**, original entrance to Ride, re-modelled 1855. (Closed off, 1914.)

**Thatched Hut** for gatekeeper,1857. (Still extant, minus thatch.)

**Gate**, 1859. (Still extant).

**Fence**, 1855, to enclose College garden.(Now a wall)

**Conifers**, planted as a group, after 1853.

**Two private houses**, 1853.Their gardens extend over the line of the old Meadow border.

**Gravel paths** and **Turf Banks**,1862, over which tents were erected for the flower Shows.

THE MAP SHOWS CHANGES MADE BETWEEN 1835 & 1862.

Areas lost are shaded. New buildings are hatched.

**The Bandstand**

A Nelson-Print from about 1865, showing a view of the Orchestra or Bandstand, looking down the main Walk. The Gardens have become an attractive woodland after nearly 80 years' growth. Some trees and shrubs have been cleared around the large tree to the left, creating a distortion in the line of the Walk. This is still visible today, even though both tree and Bandstand have long gone. The band members here wear uniforms but stand as they play, in the old-fashioned way.

It is possible that two ornamental beech trees, one of which survives, were planted at this period by the Proprietary College. Local users of Sydney Gardens will remember a large fern-leafed beech (Fagus sylvatica 'Asplenifolia') on the lawn behind the Holburne Museum, which was sadly but unavoidably felled in August 1994. The annual growth rings on the stump of this tree numbered approximately 130, giving a planting date of about 1864. This coincides with the alterations made to the gardens by the Hanoverian Band Committee, but it would also have been the 10th anniversary of the College. The 1885 OS map records that stone coffins were unearthed at this spot in 1864, indicating perhaps that digging, in order to plant a tree, accidentally uncovered the Roman burials. The second tree, a magnificent weeping beech (Fagus sylvatica pendula), happily still in place on the lawn at the front of the museum, is probably the only plant remaining from the two shrubberies which once framed the lawn, and which can be seen on the early Victorian map opposite.

In their descriptions of the Shows, the anonymous reporters of the Chronicle rise to new heights of eloquence during this period.

> *"Occasionally a railway train rushed through the crowd with a rattle, a roar and a scream, ... the windows of the carriages filled with faces, the engineer for a moment ceasing to look ahead and casting a longing, lingering look behind, while the strains of the band fell all the more sweetly on the ear as the iron horse vanished with his tramp of thunder."* (31-5-1855)

> *"... the envious imps who have of late nipped buds and blossoms with their frosty teeth ..."* (describing the chilly Spring of 1861)

> *"... the Committee made light of the roaring wind of Tuesday and erected their six tents in spite of falling branches of trees and the soaking deluge of pitiless showers. Large numbers of ladies and gentlemen braved the inclement weather and were resolved that it should not prevent their enjoyment of the floral beauties, though they had to trudge through tent-paths shoe-deep in mud."* (21-5-1863)

The most resonant passage comes in the account of a lavish musical Fete held in 1857.

> *"We never visit the Sydney Gardens without being struck with the sad havoc which has been made of the picturesque by modern improvements. Moated by the canal, trenched by the railway, the great promenade truncated by the College, the edges eaten away by residences – the Gardens are a poor shadow of themselves. They are, indeed, one of many proofs of the fact that we do not value blessings until we have lost them. When the Gardens possessed long alleys, a labyrinth, a ruin, delicious grassy glades enclosed within trees, and formed a superb wood, then they were neglected; but now that they are shorn of these attractions and have become "cabinned, cribbed, confined", the citizens are trying to make the most of them. What they are now reminds us of what they might have been – a region where could be realised all the charms of the poet's land – contemplation in shady alleys, rest on mossy banks, the music of birds, and delicious quiet amidst a population of trees."*

What comment can possibly follow this, except to feel thankful, for the writer's sake, that he is not here to see Sydney Gardens now.

# The Later 19th Century

A long period of stability now began. The financial situation fluctuates, the weather does its worst, but still the Floral Fetes keep going.

In 1870 the Rev. Francis Kilvert, a native of Hardenhuish near Chippenham, describes in his diary a visit to the Flower Show of 18th May.

> "*Heat fierce and oppressive, the flower tents like furnaces. Enormous crowds, greater it is said than were ever seen at the Bath Flower Show – attracted probably by the splendid weather and excursion trains. Not a chair to be had, but happily we had taken a camp stool ... One saw everything but the flowers. It was almost impossible to get near the roses and the police kept on saying, 'Move on, move on', so we could not stand still to admire anything a moment. I think it was a good show. The heaths, roses and azaleas were beautiful and the vegetables and strawberries fine ... It was a gay sight in the gardens, the brilliant weather, bright green grass and trees, laburnums, chestnuts, may &c in blossom, and the masses of gay pretty dresses.*"[29]

In 1874, poultry and caged birds were added to the competitive show, and placed in the fenced-off garden of the College, allowing lower admission charges to be made than for the main Floral Fete. There were nearly 1,000 entries but "*Mr. Winwood's was disqualified in consequence of his hen's combs having been painted*". The following year rabbits were added, and these too were a great success, attracting 70 entries.

As the original German personnel of the Hanoverian Band died out, the Committee renamed itself, becoming the Bath City Band and Festival Fete Committee, and later, simply the Floral Fete and Band Committee. A second band was always invited to each Fete. In 1876 the Band of the Royal Horseguards won special praise for, " *... a Handel selection, which drew folk from all over the gardens*".

Since the changes of 1855 there had been Spring and late Summer Flower Shows, and a third event in early July with music, a concert party and fireworks. In 1882 the midsummer event became a Rose Show, when the National Rose Society held its annual exhibition in Sydney Gardens, organised by the Bath Committee. This show "*afforded a mid-summer attraction to Rosarians throughout the country, as well as a capital treat for local admirers of 'The Queen of Flowers'*". There were 31 classes of cut roses, filling two large tents. About 46 varieties are mentioned by name in the report of this show, and among many now forgotten, there are a few which are still obtainable, all dating from the late 1860s:

ᴜ La France, pale pink, the first ever hybrid Tea Rose;

ᴜ Marie van Houtte, a cream Tea rose;

ᴜ Duke of Edinburgh, a bright red hybrid perpetual.

The winning entry in the class for 12 new roses included Ulrich Brunner, a light crimson hybrid Perpetual, and Mme. Isaac Pereire, the familiar deep red Bourbon Rose, both new the year before, that is, 1881[30].

## The Horticultural Tent at The Bath & West of England
## Agricultural Society's Show, Plymouth, 1853

This drawing from the *Illustrated London News* for 18th June 1853, is not of a Sydney Gardens Horticultural Show, but gives a good impression of what a large floral exhibition would have looked like. The marquee is decorated with greenery and hanging Chinese lamps, and the crowd is congested to the point of discomfort, just as described by Francis Kilvert at the Sydney Gardens Show in 1870.

**The Flying Dutchman passing under the stone bridge in Sydney Gardens**
(undated photograph)

This wide-gauge engine was used in July 1881 to bring their Highnesses the Duke & Duchess of Connaught from London, on their way to present prizes at the Royal School. The Duke was Arthur, Queen Victoria's third son. A reception was arranged for them in Sydney Gardens, involving the large marquee known as the Queen of the West, in which a dais was set up bearing a maroon velvet settee and two gilt chairs, also 800 seats and standing room for 200 spectators. The Fete Committee thought nothing of dismantling 30 or 40 feet of stone balustrade next to the railway, and constructing a temporary platform for their Highnesses to disembark. Their path from the train to the marquee was lined by *"40 quaintly-dressed little girls in white muslin, Mother Hubbard cloaks and satin-trimmed bonnets, bearing gipsy baskets containing roses with which to strew the ground"*.

The combined wide- and narrow-gauge rails in this photo would have been in place from 1872 until 1892, after which narrow-gauge won the argument, and hundreds of carriages and many engines with wide-gauge wheels ended their working lives in sad rows in the sidings at Swindon. *(Picture by courtesy of Andrew Ingram, Wisbech)*

# Liquidation

In 1891 the original 99-year lease of Sydney Gardens expired, and the financial affairs had to be wound up. The first notice appears in the *Bath Chronicle* for 8th August 1892 with a list of proprietors (or shareholders), and according to an anonymous article which purports to tell the history of the Hotel building, the winding up was a very involved process as a result of the many people who had a right to a share in the proceeds.[31]

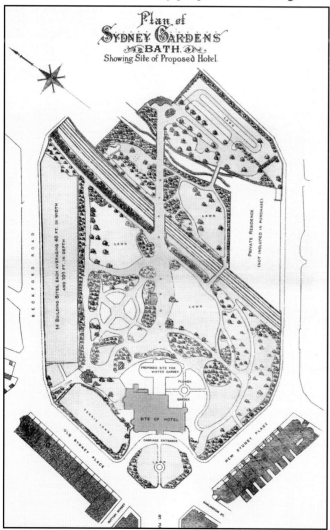

Once it was complete, the Hotel and Gardens were sold, then sold a second time, and by 1894 plans had been drawn up for a large new hotel, to be built on the site of the old, and to be financed by a new sale of shares, just like the Pleasure Gardens a century before.

The new hotel was to have 75 guest rooms, a dining room seating 150, electricity throughout, including lifts, a Winter Garden at the back, and an ornate flower garden on the south side.

**Plan of the proposed developments for Sydney Gardens**, from the flotation prospectus, 1896.
*(reproduced by kind permission of Bristol Reference Library)*

The effect that this five-storey monster would have had on the surroundings of Great Pulteney Street and Sydney Place can be imagined. Luckily there were simultaneous plans for a new hotel in the centre of Bath as well, and partly because of these, the Sydney Gardens scheme attracted few backers, and was abandoned. Thus Bath got the Empire Hotel instead, and it was Orange Grove that became permanently Victorianised, not Sydney Gardens.

THE SYDNEY GARDENS HOTEL, BATH.
FRONT AND SIDE ELEVATIONS.

**A drawing of the proposed New Hotel, 1896**. It had a Winter Garden, or heated glasshouse, extending as far as the present boundary of the Museum garden, and a large service wing out of sight on the north corner. Fourteen houses were also planned along the Beckford Road edge, where tennis and bowling now are. Today, this attempt to retain Masters' front façade while adding bay windows and French Renaissance elements, seems overdone, even a little ludicrous, and it is one of Sydney Gardens' lucky escapes that this building scheme was unsuccessful. At the time, it was not the design which exercised letter-writers to the *Bath Chronicle*. The plan to pipe hot spring water to this new hotel was seen locally as a gross unfairness when no other hotel had such a privilege, not even the Grand Pump Room Hotel which stood right opposite the Baths, and worse, not even the Mineral Water Hospital. It was eventually conceded that the hot water would be cold on arrival at the far end of Great Pulteney Street, and the idea was dropped.

# The Holburne of Menstrie Museum

The art collection of Sir William Holburne had been housed in the former Savings Bank Building in Charlotte Street, but Miss Holburne who administered her brother's affairs after his death, had ear-marked the Sydney Hotel as an ideal place for its public display as early as 1880, when the College vacated the building. Even after the Sydney Gardens lease was wound up in 1892, ten years after Miss Holburne's death, the Trustees were unable to carry out her wishes as long as the heirs to the Bathwick Estate insisted on the Hotel and Gardens being sold unseparated. This problem proved impossible to resolve until Bath City Council stepped in with what seems, with hindsight, a very obvious solution – that they would purchase the entire property and then sell the Trustees what they wanted, which was the building, the area in front, and a small garden behind.

This arrangement did not take shape until the end of 1908, and another four years were taken up with legal details. At last, by the end of 1912, the decrepit old building had new owners. Together with two acres of garden, it cost them £2,650. To repair and re-design it as a museum cost five times this figure.[32]

The exterior alterations to Harcourt Masters' original building are what concern us here. The architect Sir Reginald Blomfield was asked to create a window-less gallery with

A 1904 picture of **Harcourt Masters' Hotel**, with the extra floor of bedrooms designed by Pinch in 1836, making it a four-storey building. To the right are some extra structures put up for the Proprietary College. It had been empty and unused for over 20 years when this photograph was taken.

A recent photograph of the **Holburne Museum**. The alterations made by Sir Reginald Blomfield in 1915 can be compared with the photograph on the previous page.

top lighting for the picture collection, a second gallery for the ceramics and furniture, accommodation for a caretaker on the ground floor, and to remove the loggia and orchestra platform at the back. The front façade has in fact very slight alteration: a balustrade and vases on the roof conceal the three lantern skylights from view, and the windows are blocked up on the inside; the former second-floor windows are replaced by a pair of cartouches with garlands, very much in the style of Baldwin; and the first-floor windows are lengthened to meet the cartouches. The ground floor is not changed, but the out-buildings are cleared away and a single colonnade with balustrade joins the main building to the side screen walls.

On the Garden side the changes are drastic, because without a doorway the façade is an impersonal cliff face, and the Museum garden, while pleasant and secluded, is bereft of its original purpose as a receiving area for people spilling out of the Hotel. This sense of loss is based on nostalgia for the integrity of the first layout, as seen in Nattes' drawing on page 33, but Blomfield, when he destroyed what remained of it, was merely doing as he was asked by the Museum Trustees. It would have been an excellent thing, though, if he had made records before the demolition took place.

The alterations were complete in 1915 and the Museum opened the next year. Its garden wall extended from the curved fence put up for the College playground in 1855 down to the street boundary on both sides, involving a slight kink on the north side to accommodate a double tennis court. The public entrance on the south side was blocked off.

The Council's Parks and Cemeteries Committee began considering what needed to be done in Sydney Gardens in January 1911, after almost 20 years of neglect. Remarkably, throughout the period of changing ownership and minimal upkeep, the Flower Shows and Fetes continued as before, and were so valued, in the round of open-air events every summer, that the Band Committee was awarded a subsidy from the Mayor, as high as £700 in 1912, against its inevitable losses. The illustrations on page 57 show the Gardens during this interregnum.

In 1895 a Dog Show was added to the Poultry and Cage Birds in the old College grounds. Unfortunately the *"cries of the canine race resounded all over the Gardens"*, which, the *Chronicle* journalist conceded, could hardly be called an additional attraction. Cats were also shown, among them *"many exceedingly pretty creatures, the kittens being exceptionally taking"*.

The Rose Show of 1900 was more resplendent than ever, with the first class for Nurserymen requiring 3 trusses each of no less than 72 varieties of rose, and even for the Amateurs, the first class required 24 varieties, but only one spray of each. "La France" is still valued, and has a class to itself, which requires 12 trusses, and the only other rose having its own class is "Cloth of Gold",[30] a sulphur-yellow Noisette climber, which, the journalist recalls, used to bloom freely on the front of Wellow vicarage.

From 1909 comes an account of the music and the fireworks at the two-day Rose Show, making an interesting comparison with what Jane Austen saw and heard a century before. Selections from *Tom Jones* (Edward German), *Il Trovatore* (Verdi), *Reminiscences of Tchaikovsky*, *"embodying the finale from '1812'"* were heard, and then the Bath Military Band joined forces with the visiting Band of H.M.Lifeguards to render the Overture to Hérold's *Zampa*, a selection from *The Mikado*, which was encored, and the Introduction to Act 2 of *Lohengrin*. The fireworks began with *"a detonation that shook the earth"*, followed by the ascent of a fire balloon. Rockets shoot up, with showers of stars, *"... fiery tadpoles that over-wriggle themselves and burst after two seconds of glorious life, fantastic forms whose decline and fall are accentuated by a weird, sad whistling"*. A monkey outlined in fireworks mounts a pole, a silver waterfall cascades down, and Vesuvius erupts. Other set pieces culminated in *"the loyal finale in which Edward VII is seen gazing at a Prayer for his own Preservation"*.

The Gardens were much appreciated for their forest-like appearance, and contained *"some of the finest trees in the county"*, according to the pamphlet prepared for the flotation in 1896. The *"superb wood"* remembered by the journalist in 1857, was now described as *"a delightful sylvan retreat"*, with a *"sense of seclusion and beauty"* when compared to Victoria Park. What better place, therefore, to hold open-air performances of Shakespeare. 1890 saw *A Midsummer Night's Dream* done on the slope between the canal and railway, the audience seated on the terrace with their backs to the wall, and in 1896, what else, in this wooded setting, than the forest scenes from *As You Like It*.

**Two Views of the Entrance to Sydney Gardens in 1893**

The Gatekeeper's Hut is still there, without its decorative barge boards and its covering of ivy. The gateway was shut off when the Museum bought this area of the Gardens. The large trees have all gone; to the right of the gate the huge stump of an elm remained until the mid 1980s.

Looking in the opposite direction, the path follows the line of the original Ride, but has smooth lawns and scalloped flower beds. The wall enclosing the Museum Garden was built right across this view about 1920. *(both photographs reproduced by kind permission of Bristol Reference Library)*

# Bath City Council Takes Over

After some grumbling about the unkempt state of Sydney Gardens and how costly it was going to be to put it to rights, the Parks and Cemeteries Committee began by removing unsafe and elderly trees, and repairing the Bandstand, Loggia, swings and seating, all of which were apparently in a dangerous condition. Then it was decided to build a new entrance at the Bathwick Street corner, which would be the principal way in, now that the Museum owned the land where the former gates had been. The least expensive tenders were accepted, £219.10s. for the pillars, gatekeeper's shelter, railings and turnstile, and £70 for two wrought-iron gates, made by Singer of Frome. New paths were also laid, to accommodate the new entrance.[33]

The new path curved to meet the main Walk, leaving space for two cast-iron public conveniences, well concealed in the shrubbery. There was some discussion among the Committee as to whether cast iron was a suitable material to use in "*these beautiful old gardens, laid out with a lot of architectural skill*". Some thought that local stone would serve better to advertise the excellence of Bath's premier product for all classes of building, and would not be much more expensive. As usual, there is one member who finds the distinction "*a small point*", and cast iron prevailed, £400 being assigned for the two toilets.

Minerva's Temple was the largest project to be completed before the First World War. Designed by a local architect and based on a copy of the Roman pediment discovered in fragments near the Baths in 1790, it was intended as an advertisement for Bath at the Empire Exhibition held in the grounds of the Crystal Palace in 1911. When the Exhibition closed, the proposal was to set it up "*in some suitable spot in Bath which would best display such an ornamental structure*". With their usual sceptical tone, the Committee argued over whether it was worth £288 to Bath, this being the cost of bringing it from London. In the end it was re-erected in Sydney Gardens without its mosaic pavement, but with a plaque, paid for by the Bath Pageant Committee, who had surplus funds after their huge show in Victoria Park in 1909, and wished to have a memorial of the event.

Today the Temple sends confusing messages and is, strictly speaking, a bit of an intruder. There is no apparent link to Minerva, and the Pageant connection is contrived, since it had

---

*(right)* **Sydney Gardens photographed in 1919**

The photographer was standing at the upper window of Cleveland House, the former Kennet & Avon Canal Headquarters, which stands athwart the south tunnel on Sydney Road. The two Chinese canal bridges can be seen, also one end of the portal of the Beckford Road tunnel. Both ends of the Loggia are visible, though the centre bow is hidden. The pale surface of the footpath is striking, as it winds across the lawn between the bridges. It was later repositioned closer to the canal, and the ground to the right was banked up to accommodate the tennis courts. The telegraph poles are a sign of the utilitarian attitude which prevailed after the Gardens were run by the City Council. *(Bath Records Office)*

nothing to do with Sydney Gardens, and the Temple was not even built until two years after it had taken place. Its Roman earnestness is at odds with the spirit of the original Pleasure Garden, and its 22-foot cube is a little over-assertive for these modest-sized spaces. The remarks made by the chairman of the Parks and Cemeteries Committee at the opening ceremony on 15th June 1914 betray the contemporary line of thought. He trusts that the temple will "*stand for centuries*", and hopes that, as those concerned in the administration of Bath's parks reach their retirement, they will have "*left some footprints in the sands of time*". Unhappily, their footprints trample over earlier ones, which we would now much rather see!

The Temple was built on the site of a smaller stone shelter, seen on the 1795 map on page 6 and therefore by Thomas Baldwin, which was probably derelict by 1914, but as usual, no record was made before its demolition, not even a photograph. The cost of pulling it down and building a tool shed from the materials, was £11.10s.

The rare tree to the right of the Temple is not mentioned in the account of the opening ceremony, but must have been planted not long after. It is a hybrid Catalpa, (Catalpa erubescens), or Indian Bean Tree.

Some reminders of how things were in 1914: the gardener was paid a wage of a guinea a week, (£1.1s.), but lived rent-free in the small Lodge which still stands not far from the Bathwick Street entrance. More poignant is the letter to the Committee in September1914 from the 4th Somerset Light Infantry, saying their band would be unable to fulfill its concert contract, as the regiment had been called up to fight. By the second year of the war, lady attendants were looking after the Tennis and Bowling facilities and also collecting chair money at band concerts, their "*neat uniforms*" calling for comment by the *Chronicle* correspondent.[34] The celebrations at the end of the war included the planting of a 'Peace Oak' in Sydney Gardens by the Mayor, during a special Garden Party and Entertainment on 19th July 1919. The Oak is at the edge of the upper lawn on the north side, just by the Bowling Green. It is of course, an English Oak (Quercus robur), variety Concordia, with pale green leaves which are almost yellow when they first open in Spring.

Between the Wars, Fetes were still held, by organisations such as the Liberal Club, Twerton Co-operative Society, Bath Girl Guides, Royal United Hospital, and the British Legion, who had first to obtain consent from the Parks Committee. This was often refused, as the Fetes usually lasted three days and frequently resulted in damage to the Gardens, as well as depriving the public of free admission to what was now, nominally, their property. So the Missionary Demonstrations and the Red Cross had their Fetes but the Conservative Women's Association did not, on the grounds that it was not a charity. The Red Cross Fetes became quite rowdy, with roundabouts brought in and placed where the turf banks had been, an area soon to be made into tennis courts. This was the reason for making a new gateway opposite The Bath Spa Hotel entrance, in order to get the roundabout machinery into the Gardens.

# The Loggia and the Bandstand Meet Their Fate

The year before the Second World War found the Committee wondering what to do about the Loggia or Colonnade, which had become dangerous through lack of upkeep. Their first intention was to repair it, as it was chiefly the roof which was unsafe. There were at least two members who proposed demolition, while another said this would cause criticism, and a fourth wondered if it had "*historical associations*". Evidently the history of it was already lost, along with the identity of its architect.

The details of how the decision to rebuild part of the Loggia was arrived at are not recorded but, unsurprisingly, it was a question of finance. A tender of £1,500 had been submitted, which the Committee found too high, so the City Engineer was asked to prepare a smaller scheme. The 'smaller scheme' involved taking down the curving wings and rebuilding the centre bow, so that roughly a third of the original is left. The cost, appropriately enough, was almost exactly a third of £1,500, so the Committee adopted the lowest tender, of £447.10s. Of course there was no public consultation in 1938, and the reactions of concerned individuals, when they realised what had been done, were predictably outraged. Letters to the *Chronicle* include two outspoken complaints: Ernest Crawford of Larkhall says,

> "... *quietly and apparently without the knowledge of the members of the Bath Preservation Society (formed only the year before), this old building has been hacked down and portions rebuilt with masonry of the roughest description, a standing disgrace to a city which prides itself on fine building. But it is not only the present eyesore I decry, but the interference with the old structure, which, if in need of repair, had, at least, the merit of making a picturesque termination to a sylvan avenue.*"

Sir Ambrose Heal of the London furniture store, who had an apartment in Marlborough Buildings, sent the photograph shown on page 30 with a letter of spluttering indignation:

> "*The old pavilion had charm and elegance; it was beautifully proportioned. The suave flowing lines of its delicately moulded cornice, gently bowed in the centre and sweeping away to the incurved ends, formed a delightful terminal to the garden vista. In its simple way it was a little architectural gem. In this so-called "suitable reconstruction" the perfect proportion of the whole has been ruined. Only the centre has been preserved and the form of that has been spoilt ... We now have a bald semi-circular erection ... entirely out of scale with the whole façade of Sydney House, from which it merely bulges. Where once swept the graciously curved wings of the old pavilion are now stark, blank walls faced with cement!*"[35]

The Bath Preservation Trust addressed a letter directly to the Mayor, and since it was read to the October meeting of the Parks Committee, some of the reactions of the latter are recorded. The Trust said that while it recognised that finance had played a part in the Committee's decision, it nevertheless viewed with dismay the failure to rebuild the Loggia, and asked for reconsideration of the matter, and a new scheme for the building's completion.

The Parks Committee chairman thought the new building looked "*very nice*", and would be even better when the two sides were covered by shrubs. The Committee felt they had received undeserved abuse over the matter, believing their resolution to have been a fair one. The chairman also remarked that as Sydney Gardens was not greatly used – no band concerts were held there – he did not think the Committee were justified in spending £1,500 on the Loggia.[36]

A column in the *Chronicle* concerned with forthright comment on local affairs, signed by "*The Bellman*" (or Town Crier), takes a similar "*storm in a tea-cup*" standpoint. The Bellman finds it of no importance that "*certain curves of the old Loggia have not been reproduced*". Because the changed appearance does not conform to the original, he cannot discern anything about which to get excited.

A comparison of the Loggia today, on page 64, with the earlier one on page 30 shows that the centre bow is in fact, hardly altered at all. Perhaps the cornice is a little coarser, but this could be due to artistic license on the part of Brodribb. The step and the piers which bear two columns each, appear exactly the same as before, with their flat coping of grey pennant stone. The *amorini* or cherubs are no longer there, another complaint made by Sir Ambrose, who suspects they are on a builder's scrap heap somewhere.[37]

As well as the dumbing-down of the Loggia, two utilitarian buildings undreamt of in the original design were constructed in 1938: a wooden Tennis pavilion, and worse, the electricity sub-station, partly hidden behind a bank, close to the Sydney Place gate. Altogether, a depressing year.

Another unpopular demolition was soon being considered – this time the Victorian Orchestra or Bandstand, unused and becoming derelict by 1940. One local resident, noticing that it made a warm sun-trap in the winter months, being sheltered from the east winds, wanted permission to use it as a place to sit. The Committee felt that the staircase inside the Bandstand was unsafe, the building was too dangerous and that children would come to harm in climbing up it, especially as there were no park-keepers and the Gardens were open all night; so the request was refused. After the war there was still no move to repair it, and by 1948 the cost would have been £450, too high for the Committee to consider, so demolition was inevitable.

**The Main Walk and Bandstand, 1893.**
*(reproduced by kind permission of Bristol Reference Library)*

# The 'Bright Lights' of the 1950s

On 2nd August 1952 over 8,000 people crowded into Sydney Gardens to sample the opening night of a two-month run of special entertainments, designed not by the Parks Committee, but by the Spa Committee, in an effort to recoup the recent losses made by the Bath Assembly, forerunner of the Bath Festival. The visitors found a flood-lit wonderland, "*a grotto of greens and reds*", in the words of a *Chronicle* journalist signing himself "M.B.",

> "*Giant chestnuts, normally dark shadows against the sky, glowed in bright greens; birches and pines took on a red light, as though someone had gone over them with a tin of luminous paint and then showered sequins through the leaves.*"

On the canal,

> "*A fountain hissed a feather of spray 30 or more feet into the air. An illuminated swan with a list to port carved a stately wake through fantastic water-lilies, ignoring the brood of angular ducks which would have warmed the heart of Walt Disney.*"

There were illuminated tableaux of nursery rhymes, a mural painted on the rear wall of the Loggia, dancing to a gypsy band, and a firework display at the end. Provision of a licence for the beer tent had required special application to the licensing justices at a public hearing, where many people made strong objections to any idea of nightly entertainment in Sydney Gardens. Some thought the Spa Committee had been granted unjustified powers to do as they pleased in the Gardens, and others felt that the daytime closure for two months was not acceptable, at the height of summer. There was a petition signed by 358 local residents, while the Holburne Museum feared the show would be vulgar, and detrimental to the neighbourhood, and to Bath.

A correspondent in the *Manchester Guardian* at the end of August finds that these opposing voices are "*... a standing invitation to the comic dramatist, who might furnish a sequel to 'The Rivals' ...*". He sees the absurdity of attempting to revive the festivities of Jane Austen's time with the aim of making money, and yet protesting that "*the wrong type of people*" will descend on Bath to visit them.[38] The local journalist "M.B.", already quoted above, is less concerned with theoretical matters and writes an entertaining account of the opening night, sustaining the pleasing fantasy that Charles Harcourt Masters has returned, to show him round. "*The Ghost of Master Harcourt is happy again*", runs the headline, and, "*... looking not a day older than his 200 years*", the architect dances a jig in the middle of Sydney Place, to express his delight at the sudden popularity of "*his*" Gardens.[39]

The first night was a success, but the hoped for attendance of 20,000 each week proved to be far too optimistic. The whole season from 2nd August to 30th September attracted less than 70,000, and a loss of nearly £1,500 was made. Wet weather was blamed, the age-old enemy of Sydney Gardens entertainments. Yet the Spa Committee confidently planned another programme for 1953, arguing that the main installation work had been done, and it only needed a fine summer to produce a handsome profit.

**The Bright Lights of Sydney Gardens**

A mural of historic Bath, painted on the rear wall of the Loggia by students of the Art Secondary School, 1952.

From 1956, the fifth and last year of illuminations: the castle and the Hallowe'en scene. The wizard is on the left, the witches accompanied by owls and bats, to the right. There were also 15 illuminated episodes from *Alice in Wonderland*, a trapeze artist performing atop a 75-foot mast, and dancing on the tennis courts to the music of Laszlo Kiss and his orchestra.

New ideas in the 1953 season included a six-foot-square model of Prior Park bridge and sloping landscape garden behind, with the mansion above on its plateau. A working model of Allen's stone-hauling railway ran along one side, and the whole thing was floodlit, as were lifesize cut-outs of three 18th-century Bath figures, Ralph Allen, Beau Nash and John Wood. This year the flower beds had been planted with blooms, "whose beauty is enhanced by floodlighting", but our curiosity as to what these were is not satisfied.

One of the firework displays is evocatively described by a journalist:

> "No sooner had the flares vanished into the night when a skeleton, full of light and movement, arose from the ground and made it clear to all that in time long past he had been beheaded, for even now his head kept wandering away, but his brief spell on earth was quickly over and he disappeared as mysteriously as he had come.
>
> A great variety of rockets then soared into the air as 'Jimmy the Gymnast' limbered up for his performance. In a silver-speckled costume he twisted himself into the most amazing contortions and three times successfully heaved himself over the bar from which he was suspended. Then once more he attempted it and with great effort succeeded again. But it had been too much for him and, in his triumph, he died.
>
> Golden humming tops gyrated into the blackness and their place was taken by Catherine Wheels of great beauty. And then appeared the words 'Good Night' and high above were torrents of golden rain which dimmed and turned to autumn leaves as they fell. And then all was still. The fireworks were over, and the only light to be seen was Sham Castle, white and lonely upon the dark hillside."[40]

Thinking about this gaudy fairyland today, one tends at first to agree with Lady Noble who wrote to *The Times* from the Royal Crescent, lamenting the "*vulgarities and error of taste*" and calling the entertainments "*as remote from Jane Austen's day as can well be imagined*".[41]

But a reconstruction of the entertainments that Jane saw is not what the Spa Committee were attempting. They were anxious to "*appeal to the public taste*", and aimed no further back than the festivities of 25 to 50 years before, which several Councillors remembered. In fact, except for the use of electricity and plastic objects floating on the canal, 1952 to 1956 were much in the spirit of the early 19th century, before Galas became part of the Flower Shows.

This became even more true in 1956, when illuminated showpieces purchased from Blackpool Corporation appeared in Sydney Gardens. They included nursery rhymes like *Mary, Mary, quite contrary*, whose watering can caused her flowers to grow visibly, according to the newspaper report. (Illuminated nursery subjects had been shown at a children's fete in 1835.) There was also a 90-foot-long display called "*Hallowe'en*", which included an illuminated castle 35 feet high, "*shimmering against the night sky with a foreground of softly coloured trees and a sparkling fountain*". Also Merlin the wizard, seen in the Gardens 130 years earlier, according to Kerr;[13] three witches with cauldron; bats with ghostly whirling wings and owls with blinking eyes, all mechanical, but no doubt causing exactly the same horror as real ones did in the late 1790s. Other items in 1955 and 1956 were emphatically not like earlier times, however, such as a skittle alley and a crockery-smashing stall, and competitions for the best ankles and the most knobbly knees.

The illuminations were no longer held after 1956. Every summer had resulted in a financial short-fall, totalling more than £9,000 over the five-year period.

# Recent Changes

After so many examples of the "*sad havoc of modern improvements*", it is a pleasure in the final pages to describe one happy innovation which is not only an ornament to the scene but practical as well. The Tea House under the trees to one side of the Holburne Museum provides refreshment for today's visitors. It stands almost exactly where the 18th-century dining boxes stood, although it serves up a rather different bill of fare.

The Tea House building was originally an air-raid warden's H.Q. put up during the Second World War, using cheap, pink, mottled brick. A scheme to improve it was initiated in 1981 when the Friends of the Holburne held a competition among themselves. The winning entry, by Sidney Blackmore, suggested giving it a Gothic face-lift, and this scheme was put into practical effect by the architect David Brain. Using simple details, applied with telling skill, he transformed the unpromising structure into a light and delicate Regency Gothic garden building. The bricks disappeared beneath pink stucco, the roof acquired decorated barge boards and graceful finials, the windows have subtle tracery based on the Gothic arch, and the door has a trellis porch with pointed roof. The new Tea House opened at Easter 1983, and the following year it won an award from the Bath Conservation Area Advisory Committee. The alteration in use and in style of this building also agrees with the very spirit of a pleasure garden. Sanction for changing things around was written into the original Sydney Gardens Agreement in 1792:

*"The funds are to be used ... for erecting, building, pulling down, altering and rebuilding, orchestras, temples, seats, boxes or other buildings, ornaments and decorations proper for such gardens."*[8]

**'Before' and 'after' views of the Tea House.** It was transformed from a wartime shelter for the air-raid warden into a pretty garden house with Gothic touches.

# The Bicentenary

This brief account of Sydney Gardens will end with the 200th anniversary celebrations, held between May and September 1995.

An exhibition at the Holburne Museum traced the history of the gardens, and introduced the ideas and opinions of several present-day users, who appeared in a short video film. On display were a number of original maps and drawings, and an interesting model of the 1836 Loggia, correct in every detail, and slightly less than actual size.[42] There was also a presentation of the renovations suggested by the Debois Landscape Survey Group, who had completed their historical assessment of Sydney Gardens, commissioned by the City Council.

Outside, in the Gardens, an exhibition of structures by living artists was arranged as part of the 1995 Bath International Music Festival, under the title of *The Green Room*. Its aim, set out in an accompanying leaflet, was, "*to bring together the public, landscape architects, artists, architects and video-makers, to explore the topical issue of the nature of public open space in cities*".

In the centre of the main Walk stood *La Croix Champêtre*, a computer-generated version of a garden umbrella, sheltering chairs and tables, tea and ice cream, beneath its four humps and four down-swept eaves. It was made from lime green PVC-coated polyester on a steel frame, and specifically oriented to the compass points. It can be seen, along with other exhibits, in the photograph on page 40. In the words of the leaflet, it was, "*simultaneously a barrier, a focus, and a set of pointers*", and as such, it "*re-informs and re-works in the context of the present, our awareness of the traditions and pleasures of landscape*".[43] Alas, this recondite philosophising did not seem to persuade the habitual Sydney Gardens user to reconsider his or her feelings about the main Walk. Those who were consulted found the shelter incongruous and out of place, and their views were not the result of any historical studies, just an awareness of anachronism. And it is not just a vague 'sense of period' which is compromised here.

The main Walk was designed as a view line, initially in both directions, as well as a straight promenade, and anything placed on it or built so as to obstruct it, distorts the whole message. At best, the plastic shelter gave a cheeky prod to those at risk of taking the preservation of the Sydney Gardens design for granted. At worst, it showed the depressing need of today's artists, in a world where dis-harmony is already rampant and threatening, to present us with contrivance and controversy, almost, it seems, for their own sake. And how ironic, after 200 years of costly respect for the symmetry of the main Walk (since the construction of skew bridges is a tricky problem) to upset it on its bicentenary.

Luckily, it was but a temporary display and lasted only for the summer of 1995.

# The Future

How is Sydney Gardens to be treated as it enters its third century? What kind of pleasure garden is appropriate to our needs to-day? Do we have any obligation to the designers of 200 years ago, or are we free to forget the past and do as we like? And how much effort and money should be spent on a public area which is open at all times and which has attracted a certain amount of vandalism in recent years?

Some readers may question the assumption that the first design was automatically the best; but historically this argument must stand, because Sydney Gardens is a unique example of a Vauxhall Garden of the 18th century which is still in use as a public park. It is also of national importance as part of Baldwin's superb plan for the Pulteney's residential estate. On a more light-hearted level, it is fascinating to examine the plan of 1795 (on page 6), and try to imagine what it would have been like to wander in that garden. Of course, gardens change and grow, and the thickly-wooded Sydney Gardens of the late 19th century is no less valid, so long as the original framework is not destroyed. Even the railway did not entirely ruin it. What really caused the brave plan of 1793 to curl up and almost die, was the blocking of the main Walk at the lower end. This, together with the making of a rubbish dump to one side of it, are two unfortunate developments which will be re-thought if restoration plans go ahead.

After two articles on the re-vamping proposals had appeared in the local press (*Bath Chronicle*, 20-10-1994 and 15-5-1997), there were a few apprehensive letters from residents, who feared that the changes would be for the worse. The peace and quiet, the natural beauty of trees and flowers, were sure to be disturbed, they feared. There is no need to worry! The only things to suffer disturbance would be disfigurements like the rubbish dump, long an eye-sore behind its corrugated-iron gates, and a magnet for miscreant behaviour.

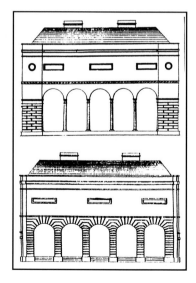

The main Walk, which is also a vista, has been blocked, first by a fence and then a wall, since the 1850s: now, wrought-iron railings with a central gate are planned, so that it will be possible to look from the Loggia down to the Museum, and on certain occasions, to walk through once again. The disused nursery area at the highest point of the Gardens has also been closed off behind gates: this would be re-designed, possibly including a castle keep to act as a vantage point, with seating for enjoying the views. An alternative to a castle is suggested on the plan opposite.

Most of the renovations on this plan are the official ones, resulting from the Survey commissioned by the then Bath City Council.[44] Suggestions made by the author of the present book are indicated with an asterisk.

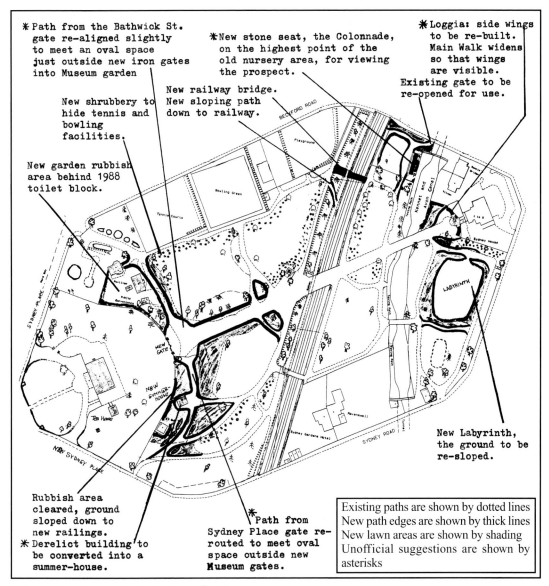

* Path from the Bathwick St. gate re-aligned slightly to meet an oval space just outside new iron gates into Museum garden

* New stone seat, the Colonnade, on the highest point of the old nursery area, for viewing the prospect.

* Loggia: side wings to be re-built. Main Walk widens so that wings are visible. Existing gate to be re-opened for use.

New shrubbery to hide tennis and bowling facilities.

New railway bridge. New sloping path down to railway.

New garden rubbish area behind 1988 toilet block.

New Labyrinth, the ground to be re-sloped.

Rubbish area cleared, ground sloped down to new railings.
* Derelict building to be converted into a summer-house.

* Path from Sydney Place gate re-routed to meet oval space outside new Museum gates.

Existing paths are shown by dotted lines
New path edges are shown by thick lines
New lawn areas are shown by shading
Unofficial suggestions are shown by asterisks

*(above)* **New Proposals for Sydney Gardens**

*(left)* **Two of Baldwin's drawings of his "*Outletts*"**, houses with arcaded shelters on the garden fronts, taken from the 1794 Indenture in Bath Records Office. One of these ground-floor colonnades could be copied for a stone seat at the highest point, where a bank already exists.

# Notes & References

All quoted material and illustrations come from Bath Reference Library unless otherwise stated, with the exception of some published works.

1   John Billingsley, *A General View of the Agriculture of the County of Somerset*, 1795. He mentions some roads in Somerset, which are "as smooth as a gravel walk", because they are formed from carefully broken stones, "*no bigger than a pigeon's egg*". The method was a vast improvement on the primitive system in use at the time, and after 1818 was adopted everywhere under McAdam's administration. John Kerr in 1825 says the Sydney Gardens Ride was "MacAdamised": but he is not referring to tarmac, as asphalt was not invented till the 1840s. The Ride and all the Walks were intended to be the colour of gravel or of Bath Stone chippings. See W.J.Reader, *Macadam, The McAdam Family & the Turnpike Roads*, Heinemann, 1980; Anthony Bird, *Roads and Vehicles*, Longmans, 1969.
2   Grosvenor Gardens is seen on Harcourt Masters' map. It is discussed in detail in my full-length book on Sydney Gardens, now in preparation.
3   Indenture of 2nd October 1794, Bath Records Office. In the mid-18th century, pleasure gardens normally had a building containing a 'Long Room', to accommodate country dances in long sets, and possible promenading in wet weather, with other rooms for dining and cards. (The Bath Assembly Rooms by the younger John Wood follows this tradition.) Sydney House, to Harcourt Masters' design, begun in November 1796, departed from the plan in having an oblong ballroom on the first floor. The first tenant, John Gale, uses the term 'House' in his opening announcements. The terms 'inn' and 'lodging house' are not used, so the assumption must be that the top-floor rooms housed the tenant and his family and perhaps kitchen and garden staff, but were not hired out to paying visitors. The term 'Tavern' is sometimes used, and 'Hotel' increasingly after 1813. By 1836 when more rooms were added, it was a hotel in the modern sense. At that point the name was changed to Pulteney Hotel, to avoid confusion with Sydney House at the eastern tip of the gardens, probably built that same year.
4   *New Bath Guide*, 1796.
5   Rev. Richard Warner, *New Guide through Bath & its Environs*, 1811.
6   Jane Root, "Thomas Baldwin: his Public Career in Bath, 1775-1793", in *Bath History*, Volume 5, 1994.
7   Notices in *Bath Chronicle*, 10-4-1794 and 24-4-1794.
8   Sydney Gardens Agreement, 1792, in *Bath Tracts*, Volume 5.
9   Sale of Bridle's effects, *Bath Chronicle*, 18-6-1831.
10  Warwick Wroth & A.E.Wroth, *The London Pleasure Gardens of the Eighteenth Century*, Macmillan, 1896.
11  Captain Mainwaring, *Annals of Bath*, page 367.
12  Piers Egan, *Walks through Bath*, 1819.
13  John Kerr, *Sydney Gardens Vauxhall, Bath. Syallabus, or descriptive representation of the numerous productions of nature and art, presented in this extensive establishment ...* , 1825.
14  Fireworks, *Rees' Cyclopaedia*, 1819, which cites 'Jones Fireworks', 1776. Also, George Plimpton, *Fireworks*, Doubleday, 1984; Anchor, 1989.
15  John Rennie, "Plan of the proposed navigable canal between the River Kennett ... and the River Avon ... ", 1793". Engraving by Faden, 1794.
16  John Nattes, *Bath, illustrated by a series of Views from the Drawings of J.C. Nattes with a description to each plate, &c.*, 1806.
17  It is sometimes stated that Stothert & Pitt manufactured the cast-iron bridges in Sydney Gardens, but this is not strictly correct. George Stothert senior (1755-1818) began his ironmongery business in Bath about 1779, as an agent and distributor of small cast-iron goods made in Coalbrookdale. These included grates, ovens, fire-backs, balusters, and railings and were sent to Bath by river. The Sydney Gardens bridges were part of this trade, undoubtedly helped along by George, who was a member of the Committee of the Pleasure Garden. The designs were chosen by the Committee from patterns sent from Coalbrookdale. Stothert's own foundry in Bath was not begun until 1815, and the two footbridges over the Kennet and Avon Canal on the Widcombe flight of locks were probably cast there shortly after. The name of Robert Pitt was not part of the firm's name until 1855. See Hugh Torrens, *The Evolution of a Family Firm – Stothert & Pitt of Bath*, 1978.
18  Quoted by James Granville Southworth, in *Vauxhall Gardens – A Chapter in the Social History of England*, Columbia University Press, 1941.
19  Tobias Smollett, *Humphrey Clinker*, 1771; Penguin Classics, 1985.

20 *The Vauxhall Observer*, 23 May, 1823.
21 *The Muses's Bower – Vauxhall Gardens 1728-1786*, Exhibition Catalogue, Gainsborough's House Museum, Sudbury, 1978.
22 *Bath Chronicle*, 10-4-1834. (The Middle Bar.)
23 Ellen Wilson, "A Shropshire Lady in Bath, 1794-1807", in *Bath History*, Volume 4, 1992. She mentions "*a very good deception painted on canvas of a stone arch*".
24 Picture from Wroth, *op. cit.*, as also are those on pages 2 and 34, lower.
25 *Bath Chronicle*, 24-4-1828. (Theft from the Aviary.)
26 *Bath Chronicle*, 10-5-1832. (Sydney Tap.)
27 Alan Mitchell, *Alan Mitchell's Trees of Britain*, Harper Collins, 1996.
28 The Wellingtonia, (*Sequoiadendron Giganteum*), introduced by Lobb in December 1853, working for Veitch of Exeter, from the Sierra Nevada, California, its only home-land. Named in honour of the hero of Waterloo who had recently died, the seedling trees were planted in hundreds by Victorian land owners, and are now lifting their tall narrow spires to 150 feet, if they escape lightning strike. See Note 27, also T. Pakenham, *Meetings with Remarkable Trees*, Weidenfeld, 1996.
29 The Rev. Frances Kilvert, *Diary*, edited by W. Plomer, Jonathan Cape, 1938, quoted by courtesy of the publisher.
30 *David Austin Roses*, catalogue for 1998.
31 *Bath Chronicle*, 27-5-1909. This anonymous piece on the history of the Sydney Hotel building contains many inaccurate statements; for example the dates given for opening and closing down are in fact those for Apollo Gardens, which were situated not far from the London Vauxhall. Also, the Harcourt Masters Tavern was not begun in 1790, but 1796. (In 1790 the whole scheme of Sydney Gardens was still a gleam in the eye of the Pulteneys, and was not set in motion until the very end of 1792.)
32 Lutz Haber, "The First 75 Years of the Holburne Museum", in *Bath History*, Volume 5, 1994.
33 Council Committee Meeting Minutes, Bath Records Office.
34 *Bath Chronicle*, 15-5-1915. (Lady Chair Attendants.)
35 *Bath Chronicle*, 31-8-1938. (Sir Ambrose Heal's letter.) The original letter is preserved in Bath Reference Library; the version printed has been considerably modified by the editor of the *Chronicle*.
36 *Bath Chronicle*, 22-10-1938. This remark, made by the Parks Committee chairman of 60 years ago, is a chilling foretaste of the attitude often adopted by councils today, and described in a recent booklet on the threat now hanging over many of our historic parks, nationwide. Low funding leads to an air of neglect, and soon there is vandalism, leading to public avoidance, which is interpreted as under-use. The next step is the assessment by councils that 'development' is a more profitable use for the open space. Indoor sports facilities are sometimes built, and in Newton Abbot, Devon, a park now has a large supermarket standing among its mature trees. The local community has erected a plaque saying, "This park was set up by public subscription and destroyed by corporate intrigue". A park in Worcester almost suffered a similar fate, the council's justification being "that people just walked through it". Local resistance was firm – is that not one of the uses for a park? The supermarket scheme was duly defeated. Happily the Lottery Fund now holds out the possibility of rescue for Public Parks, including Sydney Gardens. See Conway & Lambert, *Public Prospects – Historic Urban Parks under Threat*, The Garden History Society & The Victorian Society, 1993.
37 These two cherubs, according to a former Bath librarian, came originally from the façade of the Hart Lodgings in Stall Street. See *Bath Weekly Chronicle*, 10-9-1938. The librarian gave no source for this information, but the Hart Lodging cherubs certainly look the same as the ones on the Loggia, and it was the Sydney Gardens architect Thomas Baldwin who was building the new Baths entrance on this site in 1787 after the lodgings were pulled down. It was a late Tudor building, so the two ornaments, which can be seen to have lost their arms by the time Brodribb drew them in 1936, were probably past repair when it came to the 1938 reconstruction.
38 Article by Kenneth Gregory, *Manchester Guardian*, 27-8-1952.
39 The Ghost of Master Harcourt, *Bath Weekly Chronicle*, 4-8-1952.
40 Firework display, *Western Morning Press*, 11-9-1953.
41 Lady Noble's letter, *The Times*, 7-8-1953. Reprinted in the *Bath Critic*, September 1953, with subsequent correspondence.
42 The exhibition, "Views on Sydney Gardens, The story of the Pleasure Gardens from 1795-1995", was organised by Sue Swingler. The Loggia was re-constructed by Kevin Plumley.
43 Quoted from *The Green Room, Sydney Gardens, Bath. Views on an 18th Century Pleasure Ground*, a brochure published in May 1995 by the Bath Festivals Trust. The Green Room Exhibiton was conceived and directed by

Caryn Faure Walker, Faculty of Art, Media & Design, University of the West of England. Buro Happold built the Croix to a design by Nigel Coates.

44 *Sydney Gardens, Bath: A Survey of the Landscape*, Colvin & Moggridge and Debois Landscape Survey Group, Summary, December 1992, revised April 1993, unpublished.

# Acknowledgements

My biggest debt of gratitude is due to Bath Reference Library and its staff, ever helpful and ever tolerant of my increasingly complex inquiries. Special thanks to Liz Bevan for help with the illustrations. The staff of Bath Records Office were also unfailingly courteous, and helpful far beyond the call of duty. I acknowledge with thanks, a small grant from the Garden History Society, and further help from Mavis Batey, its president. Many people have been generous with their special knowledge or advice: Peter Atkinson, Trevor Fawcett, Kenneth Gregory, Dr. Stewart Harding, Glenn Humphreys, David Lambert, the late Joanne Leslie, Adrienne Lewis, John Phibbs, Peggy Stembridge, and Jane Whyberd. Several people have read early versions of the book and offered useful comment: Pam and Colin Booth, Susan and Ian Fraser, Elspeth and Martin Read. Juliet Greaves has produced charming art work, and Jo Young has provided word-processing skills more than equal to the author's finicky demands. Thanks to all of them, and lastly to the users of Sydney Gardens who have, knowingly or unawares, been the subjects of my photographs. While every effort has been made to credit illustrative material accurately, I offer my apologies to anybody who may have been overlooked.

# Request for Photographs

This is a plea to readers who may have pre-first world war pictures of Sydney Gardens, to let me see them. It is frustrating that no photos of the flower shows, for example, appear to have survived in the public collections. Photos sent care of the publisher, will be gratefully acknowledged, and returned unharmed.